OLYMPIC GAMES PARIS 2024

The Ultimate Handbook for the 2024 Summer Olympics

Brian Phil

All Rights Reserved. No part of this publication may be produced, stored or transmitted in any form or by any means, electronic, mechanical, photocopying, recording, scanning or otherwise without written permission from the publisher. It is illegal to copy his book, post it to a website, or distribute it by any other means without permission.

Copyright © Brian Phil 2024

TABLE OF CONTENTS

INTRODUCTION 7
- OVERVIEW OF THE 2024 OLYMPICS 7
- HISTORICAL SIGNIFICANCE 8
- GOALS AND THEMES FOR 2024 9

CHAPTER ONE 13
- HISTORY OF PARIS AS A HOST CITY 13
- KEY VENUES AND FACILITIES 14
- CULTURAL HIGHLIGHTS AND TOURIST ATTRACTIONS 19

CHAPTER TWO 25
- ORGANIZATIONAL STRUCTURE 25
- INTERNATIONAL OLYMPIC COMMITTEE (IOC) 25
- LOCAL ORGANIZING COMMITTEE 27
- VOLUNTEER AND STAFF INVOLVEMENT 29
- PARTNERSHIPS AND SPONSORSHIPS 32

CHAPTER THREE 43
- SPORTS AND DISCIPLINES 43
- OVERVIEW OF OLYMPIC SPORTS 43
- NEW AND RETURNING SPORTS 46
- SCHEDULE OF EVENTS 49
- VENUE LOCATIONS FOR EACH SPORT 53

CHAPTER FOUR 59
- ATHLETES TO WATCH 59
- PROFILES OF TOP CONTENDERS 59
- RISING STARS AND NEWCOMERS 63
- DIVERSITY AND INCLUSION IN THE ATHLETE POOL 67

CHAPTER FIVE 71
- OPENING AND CLOSING CEREMONIES 71
- THEMES AND HIGHLIGHTS OF THE OPENING CEREMONY 71
- KEY PERFORMANCES AND MOMENTS 73

3

CULTURAL SIGNIFICANCE AND SYMBOLISM IN THE CLOSING CEREMONY 80

CHAPTER SIX 85

MEDAL EVENTS 85
MEDAL TALLY AND LEADERBOARD 85
HISTORIC MEDAL WINS AND RECORDS 86
COUNTRY-BY-COUNTRY BREAKDOWN 88
INSPIRATIONAL STORIES OF TRIUMPH 93

CHAPTER SEVEN 99

MEMORABLE MOMENTS 99
HISTORIC ACHIEVEMENTS AND RECORDS 99
UNFORGETTABLE PERFORMANCES 102
CONTROVERSIES AND CHALLENGES 104

CHAPTER EIGHT 107

TECHNOLOGY AND INNOVATION 107
TECHNOLOGICAL ADVANCES IN SPORTS 107
SUSTAINABILITY INITIATIVES AND GREEN TECHNOLOGY 110
SAFETY AND SECURITY MEASURES 112
TECHNOLOGICAL INNOVATIONS ENHANCING THE OLYMPIC EXPERIENCE 115

CHAPTER NINE 123

IMPACT ON HOST CITY 123
ECONOMIC IMPACT AND TOURISM 123
URBAN DEVELOPMENT AND INFRASTRUCTURE LEGACY 126
SOCIAL AND CULTURAL INFLUENCE 129
ECONOMIC IMPACT: A CLOSER LOOK 131

CHAPTER TEN 135

FAN EXPERIENCE 135
TICKETING AND ACCESS INFORMATION 135
FAN ZONES AND VIEWING AREAS 138
MERCHANDISE AND SOUVENIRS 140

CHAPTER ELEVEN 149

OLYMPIC VILLAGE..149
ACCOMMODATION AND FACILITIES FOR ATHLETES 149
DAILY LIFE IN THE OLYMPIC VILLAGE 152
SECURITY AND HEALTH MEASURES...155

CHAPTER TWELVE...161

APPENDICES 161
GLOSSARY OF TERMS...161
DETAILED EVENT SCHEDULE 169

CONCLUSION 175

INTRODUCTION

Welcome to the thrilling journey of the 2024 Olympic Games!

If you've ever felt the surge of excitement while watching athletes push the boundaries of human potential, you're in the right place. The Olympics are more than just a series of competitions; they're a celebration of our shared humanity, resilience, and the indomitable spirit that drives us to be our best. This book is your ticket to exploring every facet of the upcoming 2024 Games – from the grand overview and historical significance to the ambitious goals and captivating themes that will shape this monumental event. Whether you're a sports enthusiast, a curious observer, or someone who loves a good story of triumph and perseverance, there's something here for you.

Overview of the 2024 Olympics

The 2024 Olympic Games, officially known as the Games of the XXXIII Olympiad, are set to take place in the vibrant city of Paris, France.

Paris will now host the Summer Olympics for the third time, having done so twice before in 1900 and 1924. The choice of Paris as the host city was announced on September 13, 2017, following a competitive bidding process. With its rich history, iconic landmarks, and a global reputation for art and culture, Paris promises to offer a unique backdrop for the Games.

The 2024 Olympics will bring together over 10,000 athletes from more than 200 countries, competing in a diverse array of sports. From traditional events like athletics, swimming, and gymnastics to newer additions such as skateboarding, surfing, and sport climbing, the Games will showcase the breadth and depth of athletic talent from around the world. Paris has committed to delivering a spectacular and sustainable event, emphasizing innovation, inclusivity, and environmental responsibility.

As you prepare to dive into the details of each sport and the athletes to watch, it's essential to understand the broader context of the 2024 Olympics. This edition of the Games is poised to be a turning point in Olympic history, setting new standards for how mega-events can inspire, engage, and positively impact our global community.

Historical Significance

The Olympics have always been a reflection of their times, capturing the spirit, challenges, and aspirations of the world at large. The 2024 Olympics are no exception. As we gather in Paris, we're reminded of the profound historical significance of these Games.

The modern Olympic movement, revived by Pierre de Coubertin in 1896, was inspired by the ancient Greek tradition of athletic competitions held in Olympia. These early Games were a celebration of physical prowess, unity, and peace – values that remain at the core of the modern Olympics. The 2024 Games will celebrate the 100th anniversary of the last Paris Olympics in 1924, offering a poignant link to the past while looking firmly towards the future.

In the century since the 1924 Paris Olympics, the world has undergone immense changes. We've witnessed the rise and fall of empires, the triumphs of civil rights movements, and the exponential growth of technology and globalization. Throughout these changes, the Olympics have served as a beacon of hope and unity, bringing together people from diverse backgrounds to celebrate our common humanity.

The Paris 2024 Games will also highlight the historical significance of gender equality and inclusivity in sports. With an equal number of events for men and women, the 2024 Olympics will be the most gender-balanced in history. This commitment to equality reflects broader societal shifts towards recognizing and celebrating the achievements of all athletes, regardless of gender.

Goals and Themes for 2024

Every Olympic Games has a set of overarching goals and themes that guide its planning and execution. The 2024 Olympics are no different, with a clear vision aimed at creating a lasting legacy for Paris, France, and the world.

One of the primary goals of the 2024 Olympics is to deliver a sustainable and environmentally responsible event. In an era where climate change and environmental degradation are pressing global issues, the organizers have pledged to minimize the carbon footprint of the Games. This commitment includes the use of renewable energy sources, sustainable construction practices, and initiatives to reduce waste and promote recycling. By setting new standards for sustainability, the Paris 2024 Games aim to inspire future hosts to prioritize environmental stewardship.

Another key theme of the 2024 Olympics is inclusivity. The Games will be a platform to celebrate diversity and promote social cohesion. This includes efforts to ensure accessibility for athletes and spectators with disabilities, as well as initiatives to engage underrepresented communities. The Paris 2024 organizing committee is dedicated to making the Games a truly inclusive event where everyone feels welcome and valued.

Innovation is also at the heart of the 2024 Olympics. Paris plans to leverage cutting-edge technology to enhance the experience for athletes, spectators, and viewers around the world. From advanced broadcasting techniques that bring the action closer to home to the use of artificial intelligence and data analytics to improve athlete performance, the 2024 Games will showcase the latest in sports technology.

Furthermore, the 2024 Olympics will emphasize the importance of legacy. The organizers are focused on creating long-term benefits for the host city and its residents. This includes the development of new sports facilities and infrastructure, as well as initiatives to promote physical activity and healthy lifestyles among Parisians. The legacy of the 2024

Games will extend beyond the two weeks of competition, leaving a lasting impact on the city and its people.

Finally, the 2024 Olympics will celebrate the rich cultural heritage of Paris and France. The Games will be an opportunity to showcase French art, music, cuisine, and traditions to a global audience. From the opening ceremony to the various cultural events planned throughout the Games, Paris will share its unique charm and elegance with the world.

As we embark on this journey through the 2024 Olympic Games, you'll gain a deeper understanding of the athletes' stories, the significance of each sport, and the broader impact of this remarkable event. You'll learn about the challenges and triumphs that define the Olympic experience, and you'll be inspired by the dedication and perseverance of the athletes who strive for greatness.

The 2024 Olympics are more than just a series of competitions; they're a testament to the power of sport to unite us, inspire us, and drive positive change. So, let's dive in and explore the magic of the 2024 Games together. Welcome to the world of the Olympics – where dreams are realized, records are broken, and history is made.

CHAPTER ONE

History of Paris as a Host City

Paris is a city with a rich tapestry of history, culture, and, of course, sporting excellence. As we embark on this journey to explore the 2024 Olympic Games, let's explore Paris's vibrant past as a host city.

Paris, often referred to as "The City of Light," has a long and illustrious history with the Olympic Games. This isn't the first time Paris has rolled out the red carpet for the world's best athletes. In fact, Paris has hosted the Summer Olympics twice before: in 1900 and 1924.

The 1900 Summer Olympics, also known as the Games of the II Olympiad, were a unique affair. They were held as part of the 1900 Exposition Universelle, a world's fair celebrating the achievements of the 19th century and looking forward to the new century. These games were quite different from what we know today. There were no opening or closing ceremonies, and many athletes didn't even realize they were competing in the Olympics! Despite this, it was a significant milestone for Parisand the Olympic movement.

Fast forward to 1924, and Paris was ready to host the Games of the VIII Olympiad. These games were much more recognizable to us today, with organized ceremonies, a dedicated Olympic Village, and a full schedule of events. The 1924 Olympics are perhaps best remembered for the stunning performances and the introduction of the Olympic motto: "Citius, Altius, Fortius" (Faster, Higher, Stronger). It was a time of post-war recovery and optimism, and Paris shone brightly on the global stage.

Now, nearly a century later, Paris is once again preparing to host the Summer Olympics. The city has undergone significant changes and developments, making it an ideal location for the 2024 Games. As we delve deeper into this chapter, we'll explore the key venues and facilities, the extensive infrastructure and preparations, and the cultural highlights that make Paris a perfect host city.

Key Venues and Facilities

Hosting the Olympic Games is no small feat, and Paris has pulled out all the stops to ensure that athletes and spectators alike have an unforgettable experience. The city boasts a mix of historic and state-of-the-art venues, each chosen to highlight Paris's unique charm and enhance the overall Olympic experience.

Stade de France

Let's start with the Stade de France, the centerpiece of the 2024 Olympic Games. Located in the suburb of Saint-Denis, this iconic stadium has a seating capacity of over 80,000 and will host the opening and closing ceremonies, as well as athletics events. The Stade de France has a storied history, having hosted the 1998 FIFA World Cup final and numerous other major sporting events. Its modern design and excellent facilities make it the perfect venue for showcasing the world's top athletes.

Roland Garros

Next up is Roland Garros, famous for the French Open tennis tournament. This historic venue will host the tennis events during the Olympics. With its clay courts and intimate seating, Roland Garros offers a unique and prestigious setting for Olympic tennis. Imagine watching a thrilling match with the Eiffel Tower in the distance—it's a sight you won't want to miss!

Parc des Princes

For football fans, the Parc des Princes will be a highlight. Home to Paris Saint-Germain (PSG), one of Europe's top football clubs, this stadium will host football matches throughout the Olympics. With its passionate fans and electric atmosphere, the Parc des Princes promises to deliver unforgettable moments on the pitch.

Champ de Mars

One of the most iconic locations in Paris, the Champ de Mars, located right beneath the Eiffel Tower, will be transformed into a temporary venue for beach volleyball. Picture this: athletes diving for the ball with the Eiffel Tower as their backdrop. It's a quintessentially Parisian experience that perfectly blends sport and culture.

Grand Palais

The Grand Palais, with its stunning Beaux-Arts architecture, will host fencing events. This historic venue, built for the 1900 Exposition Universelle, has been beautifully preserved and modernized, making it an ideal location for showcasing the elegance and precision of fencing.

Bercy Arena

For basketball enthusiasts, the Bercy Arena (AccorHotels Arena) is the place to be. This multi-purpose indoor arena has a capacity of over 20,000 and will host basketball and gymnastics events. Its central location and excellent facilities ensure that both athletes and fans will have a top-notch experience.

Palais des Sports

The Palais des Sports will host the weightlifting competitions. This venue, known for its excellent acoustics and intimate atmosphere, will allow spectators to feel close to the action as athletes push their limits and break records.

Versailles

A nod to the grandeur of French history, the Palace of Versailles will host the equestrian events. The stunning gardens and historic buildings provide a breathtaking backdrop for dressage, show jumping, and eventing. It's a perfect blend of history and sport that highlights the unique character of the 2024 Olympics.

Infrastructure and Preparations

Hosting the Olympics requires meticulous planning and extensive preparations. Paris has left no stone unturned in its efforts to ensure that the 2024 Games are a resounding success. From transportation to sustainability, let's take a closer look at the infrastructure and preparations that are transforming the city.

Transportation

Getting around Paris during the Olympics will be a breeze, thanks to a comprehensive transportation plan. The city has invested heavily in expanding and upgrading its public transportation network. The Paris Métro, known for its efficiency and extensive coverage, will be the backbone of this plan. New lines and extensions are being added to ensure that all key venues are easily accessible.

In addition to the Métro, the Réseau Express Régional (RER) trains will provide rapid transit to and from the suburbs. The high-speed TGV trains will connect Paris with other major cities in France and Europe, making it easy for international visitors to travel to the Games. To further enhance mobility, Paris is also expanding its network of bike lanes and pedestrian-friendly zones, encouraging eco-friendly transportation options.

Accommodation

Paris is well-equipped to handle the influx of visitors expected during the Olympics. The city boasts a wide range of accommodation options, from luxury hotels to budget-friendly hostels and charming boutique hotels. The Olympic Village, located in the Seine-Saint-Denis area, will house the athletes and provide them with state-of-the-art facilities. This purpose-built village will ensure that athletes have everything they need to perform at their best, from training facilities to medical care and recreational areas.

Sustainability

One of the key pillars of the 2024 Olympics is sustainability. Paris is committed to hosting the most environmentally friendly Games in history. This commitment is evident in every aspect of the planning and execution of the event. For instance, the majority of the venues are existing facilities, reducing the need for new construction and minimizing the environmental impact.

Renewable energy sources will power the venues, and a comprehensive recycling program will be in place to manage waste. The city is also promoting sustainable transportation options, such as electric buses and bikes, to reduce carbon emissions. Furthermore, Paris is working closely with local communities to ensure that the benefits of hosting the Olympics extend beyond the Games themselves, leaving a positive legacy for future generations.

Security

The safety and security of athletes, officials, and spectators is a major priority.

Paris has a robust security plan in place, developed in collaboration with international security experts. This plan includes advanced surveillance systems, increased police presence, and comprehensive emergency response protocols. The city's experience in hosting large-scale events, such as the UEFA Euro 2016, has provided valuable insights and lessons that will be applied to the Olympics.

Cultural Highlights and Tourist Attractions

No trip to Paris would be complete without exploring its rich cultural heritage and world-famous attractions. Whether you're a history buff, an art lover, or a foodie, Paris has something to offer evcryone. Let's take a look at some of the must-see sights and experiences that will make your visit to the 2024 Olympics truly unforgettable.

Eiffel Tower

Standing tall and proud, the Eiffel Tower is the symbol of Paris. This famous landmark offers stunning and mind-blowing views of the city from its observation decks. Whether you choose to take the elevator or climb the stairs, the experience is nothing short of magical. And don't forget to visit at night, when the tower is beautifully illuminated, casting a romantic glow over the city.

Louvre Museum

Home to thousands of works of art, including the Mona Lisa and the Venus de Milo, the Louvre Museum is a treasure trove of artistic masterpieces. Spend a day wandering through its vast galleries, and you'll discover a world of beauty and history. The Louvre's glass pyramid entrance is an architectural marvel in itself, seamlessly blending the old with the new.

Notre-Dame Cathedral

Although it suffered a devastating fire in 2019, Notre-Dame Cathedral remains a testament to Gothic architecture and the resilience of Paris. Restoration efforts are underway, and the cathedral is expected to regain its former glory. Even in its current state, Notre-Dame is a must-visit, with its stunning façade, intricate sculptures, and awe-inspiring interior.

Montmartre

Montmartre is the place to go if you want to experience bohemian Paris.

This charming neighborhood, perched on a hill, has long been a haven for artists and writers. Stroll through its narrow streets, visit the iconic Sacré-Cœur Basilica, and enjoy the lively atmosphere of Place du Tertre, where local artists display their works. Montmartre offers a glimpse into the artistic soul of Paris.

Seine River Cruise

A cruise along the Seine River is a fantastic way to see the city's most famous landmarks from a different perspective. Relax on a boat as you glide past the Eiffel Tower, Notre-Dame, the Louvre, and more. Many cruises offer dinner and live entertainment, making it a delightful experience that combines sightseeing with a touch of romance.

Champs-Élysées

The Champs-Élysées is arguably the most famous avenue in the world. Stretching from the Arc de Triomphe to Place de la Concorde, this grand boulevard is lined with trees, shops, cafes, and theaters. It's a wonderful place for a leisurely stroll, some high-end shopping, or simply soaking up the Parisian atmosphere. Don't miss the spectacular view from the top of the Arc de Triomphe, which offers a panoramic vista of the city.

Musée d'Orsay

Housed in a stunning Beaux-Arts railway station, the Musée d'Orsay is a haven for lovers of Impressionist and Post-Impressionist art. Here, you can admire masterpieces by Monet, Van Gogh, Degas, and many others. The museum's unique architecture and its extensive collection make it a must-visit for any art enthusiast.

Luxembourg Gardens

If you're looking for a peaceful escape from the hustle and bustle of the city, the Luxembourg Gardens offer a tranquil retreat. Located in the heart of the Left Bank, these beautifully landscaped gardens are perfect for a leisurely walk, a picnic, or just relaxing by the fountains. The gardens also feature statues, flowerbeds, and the picturesque Luxembourg Palace, home to the French Senate.

Le Marais

Le Marais is one of Paris's oldest and most charming neighborhoods. Known for its narrow medieval streets, historic buildings, and vibrant atmosphere, it's a great place to explore on foot. The area is also famous for its eclectic mix of boutiques, galleries, cafes, and lively nightlife. Be sure to visit the Place des Vosges, Paris's oldest planned square, and the stunning Hôtel de Ville.

Latin Quarter

The Latin Quarter is synonymous with intellectual and artistic life. This historic district is home to the Sorbonne University and has been a center of learning since the Middle Ages. Wander through its lively streets, discover quaint bookshops like Shakespeare and Company, and enjoy a coffee in one of its many cafes. The Pantheon, where many of France's great minds are buried, is also located here.

Gastronomy

Paris is a food lover's paradise, offering everything from Michelin-starred restaurants to cozy bistros and bustling markets. Be sure to indulge in classic French cuisine, such as escargot, coq au vin, and crème brûlée. Visit the famous patisseries for a taste of exquisite pastries like macarons and éclairs. And don't forget to explore the city's vibrant food markets, such as Marché d'Aligre or Marché des Enfants Rouges, where you can sample fresh produce, cheeses, and charcuterie.

Final Thoughts

Paris is not just a city; it's an experience. The 2024 Olympic Games will not only showcase the pinnacle of athletic achievement but also the unique beauty, culture, and spirit of this magnificent city. From its historic venues and world-class facilities to its rich cultural heritage and culinary delights, Paris offers an unparalleled setting for the Olympic Games. As you prepare to attend or follow the 2024 Olympics, take the time to immerse yourself in all that Paris has to offer. Explore its iconic landmarks, savor its culinary delights, and soak up the vibrant atmosphere. Whether you're cheering on your favorite athletes, discovering the city's hidden gems, or simply enjoying the camaraderie of the global community, the 2024 Paris Olympics promise to be an unforgettable experience.

So, let the games begin, and let the magic of Paris captivate you!

CHAPTER TWO
Organizational Structure

This chapter looks into the core of the 2024 Olympic Games—the complex web of organizations, committees, volunteers, and partnerships that make this global event possible.

From the International Olympic Committee to the local volunteers, every role is crucial in bringing the Olympics to life. This chapter examines the organizational structure behind the 2024 Paris Olympics, providing you with an insider's view of the people and processes driving this monumental event.

International Olympic Committee (IOC)

At the top of the Olympic hierarchy is the International Olympic Committee (IOC). Founded in 1894, the IOC is a not-for-profit independent international organization responsible for overseeing the Olympic Movement, which includes both the Summer and Winter Games. But what exactly does the IOC do, and how does it influence the Olympics you'll witness in Paris?

The Role of the IOC

The IOC's primary role is to promote Olympism and to ensure the regular celebration of the Olympic Games. This means not only choosing the host city but also setting the rules and guidelines for the Games, ensuring fair play, and promoting the Olympic values of excellence, friendship, and respect.

Selection of the Host City

One of the most critical responsibilities of the IOC is selecting the host city. The selection process is rigorous and highly competitive, involving multiple stages and intense scrutiny. Cities interested in hosting the Games submit detailed bids outlining their vision, plans, and capabilities. These bids are reviewed and evaluated by the IOC, which considers factors such as infrastructure, accommodations, financial guarantees, and the legacy the Games will leave behind.

Paris was awarded the 2024 Olympics after a competitive bidding process that saw it triumph over several other cities. The IOC recognized Paris's strong proposal, which emphasized sustainability, existing infrastructure, and a commitment to promoting Olympic values.

Ensuring Fair Play and Integrity

The IOC is also responsible for maintaining the integrity of the Games. This includes enforcing anti-doping regulations, ensuring fair competition, and upholding the Olympic Charter. The World Anti-Doping Agency (WADA), established by the IOC, plays a crucial role in this, working to eliminate doping from sports through stringent testing and education programs.

Promoting Olympic Values

Beyond the logistical and regulatory aspects, the IOC is deeply committed to promoting the core values of the Olympic Movement. These values—excellence, friendship, and respect—are at the heart of every decision and action taken by the IOC. They aim to use sport to promote peace, inclusivity, and positive change worldwide.

Local Organizing Committee

While the IOC sets the stage, it's the Local Organizing Committee (LOC) that brings the vision to life on the ground. For the 2024 Paris Olympics, the LOC, known as Paris 2024, is the driving force behind the planning and execution of the Games. Let's explore how Paris 2024 operates and its key responsibilities.

Formation and Structure

Paris 2024 was formed shortly after Paris was awarded the Games. The committee comprises representatives from various sectors, including government officials, sports organizations, business leaders, and community representatives. This diverse group ensures that all aspects of French society are considered in the planning and execution of the Games.

Leadership

At the helm of Paris 2024 is a leadership team dedicated to ensuring the success of the Games. The President of Paris 2024, Tony Estanguet, a three-time Olympic gold medalist in canoe slalom, brings invaluable experience and passion to the role. Under his leadership, the committee works tirelessly to meet the high standards set by the IOC and to deliver a memorable and impactful event.

Key Responsibilities

Paris 2024 is responsible for a wide range of tasks, all critical to the successful hosting of the Olympics. These responsibilities include:

- ***Infrastructure Development:*** Ensuring that all venues and facilities are ready and meet the required standards.

- ***Transportation and Logistics:*** Developing a comprehensive transportation plan to facilitate the smooth movement of athletes, officials, and spectators.

- ***Security:*** Implementing robust security measures to ensure the safety of everyone involved.

- ***Community Engagement:*** Engaging with local communities to ensure their support and involvement in the Games.

- ***Sustainability:*** Promoting and implementing sustainable practices to minimize the environmental impact of the Games.

Legacy Planning

A key focus for Paris 2024 is the legacy that the Games will leave behind. This includes not only physical infrastructure but also social and economic impacts. The committee is dedicated to ensuring that the benefits of hosting the Olympics extend well beyond the closing ceremony. This includes promoting sports and healthy lifestyles, improving local infrastructure, and boosting the economy through tourism and global exposure.

Volunteer and Staff Involvement

One of the most remarkable aspects of the Olympic Games is the sheer number of people who come together to make it all happen. From seasoned professionals to enthusiastic volunteers, the human element is what truly drives the success of the Olympics. Let's take a closer look at the roles and contributions of volunteers and staff in the 2024 Paris Olympics.

Recruitment and Training

Recruiting volunteers is a massive undertaking, but it's also one of the most rewarding aspects of organizing the Olympics. Paris 2024 aims to recruit tens of thousands of volunteers from all walks of life, bringing together a diverse and dedicated team to support the Games. The recruitment process involves an extensive application and selection process to ensure that volunteers are well-suited to their roles.

Once selected, volunteers undergo rigorous training to prepare them for their tasks. This training covers a wide range of topics, including customer service, event operations, safety protocols, and cultural sensitivity. The goal is to ensure that every volunteer is equipped with the knowledge and skills needed to provide the best possible experience for athletes, officials, and spectators.

Roles and Responsibilities

Volunteers play a crucial role in every aspect of the Olympics, performing a variety of tasks that ensure the smooth operation of the Games. Some of the key roles include:

- *Event Operations:* Assisting with the setup and management of venues, ensuring that events run smoothly and on schedule.

- *Athlete Support:* Providing assistance to athletes, including transportation, logistics, and language support.

- *Spectator Services:* Helping spectators with information, directions, and any other needs to enhance their experience.

- *Media and Communications:* Supporting media operations, including assisting journalists, managing press conferences, and facilitating interviews.

- *Medical and First Aid:* Providing medical assistance and support to athletes, officials, and spectators.

The Volunteer Experience

Being a volunteer at the Olympics is a once-in-a-lifetime experience. It offers a unique opportunity to be part of a global event, meet people from around the world, and contribute to something truly special. Volunteers often form lasting friendships and create memories that they cherish forever. The sense of camaraderie and shared purpose is palpable, and the energy and enthusiasm of the volunteers are infectious.

Staff and Professional Involvement

In addition to volunteers, the Olympics rely heavily on a dedicated team of professional staff. These individuals bring a wealth of expertise and experience to their roles, ensuring that every aspect of the Games is managed efficiently and effectively. From event planners and logistics experts to security personnel and medical professionals, the staff plays a critical role in the success of the Olympics.

Internship Programs

Paris 2024 also offers internship programs for students and young professionals, providing them with valuable hands-on experience in event management, sports administration, and other related fields. These internships offer a unique opportunity to learn from industry experts and gain practical skills that can be applied to future careers.

Partnerships and Sponsorships

The Olympics are a massive undertaking, requiring significant financial resources and support from various stakeholders. Partnerships and sponsorships play a crucial role in providing the necessary funding and resources to make the Games possible. Let's explore how these partnerships are formed and the impact they have on the 2024 Paris Olympics.

The Role of Sponsors

Sponsorship is a vital component of the Olympic Games, providing essential funding and resources that support every aspect of the event. Sponsors are typically major corporations that enter into partnerships with the IOC and the local organizing committee to support the Games financially and through in-kind contributions.

Types of Sponsorships

There are several levels of sponsorships, each offering different benefits and opportunities for companies:

- **Worldwide Olympic Partners:** These are the top-tier sponsors that support the Olympic Movement on a global scale. They receive exclusive marketing rights and extensive visibility across all Olympic platforms. Examples of worldwide Olympic partners include Coca-Cola, Visa, and Samsung.

- **Official Partners:** These sponsors provide significant support to the local organizing committee and receive substantial branding and marketing opportunities within the host country. They play a crucial role in supporting the infrastructure and operations of the Games.

- ***Official Suppliers and Providers:*** These companies supply goods and services necessary for the successful execution of the Games. This can include everything from sports equipment and uniforms to technology and transportation services.

Benefits of Sponsorship

For sponsors, partnering with the Olympics offers numerous benefits. It provides a unique platform to showcase their brand on a global stage, reaching billions of viewers worldwide. The association with the Olympic values of excellence, friendship, and respect enhances the sponsor's brand image and credibility. Additionally, sponsors often engage in various marketing and promotional activities that leverage their Olympic partnership to boost sales and customer engagement.

Impact on the Games

Sponsorships have a profound impact on the success of the Olympics. The financial support from sponsors helps cover the substantial costs of hosting the Games, including venue construction, transportation, security, and more. In-kind contributions, such as technology, equipment, and services, are equally important, ensuring that the Games run smoothly and efficiently.

Collaborations and Innovations

Sponsorships often lead to exciting collaborations and innovations. For example, technology partners may introduce cutting-edge solutions to enhance the viewing experience for fans, such as augmented reality features or advanced broadcasting technologies. Sustainability partners might develop eco-friendly initiatives that reduce the environmental footprint of the Games. These collaborations not only benefit the Olympics but also drive progress and innovation in various industries.

Local Partnerships

While global sponsors provide substantial support, local partnerships are equally vital for the success of the 2024 Paris Olympics. These partnerships often involve collaboration with regional businesses, government agencies, and community organizations. Local partners play a crucial role in ensuring that the Games reflect the host city's unique character and values, and they contribute significantly to the overall experience for athletes, visitors, and residents.

Government and Public Sector Involvement

The French government and local authorities are deeply involved in the planning and execution of the Paris Olympics. This collaboration is essential for managing public infrastructure, security, transportation, and other logistical aspects. Government support also helps in securing funding for critical projects and ensuring that the Games align with national and local development goals.

For instance, the City of Paris and the Île-de-France region have committed significant resources to enhance public transportation, improve urban infrastructure, and promote sustainable initiatives. These efforts are aimed not only at facilitating the smooth operation of the Games but also at leaving a lasting positive impact on the city and its residents.

Community Organizations and Cultural Institutions

Engaging local community organizations and cultural institutions is a key aspect of the Paris 2024 strategy. By involving these groups, the organizers aim to create a more inclusive and culturally rich Olympic experience. Local artists, performers, and cultural ambassadors are being invited to participate in the opening and closing ceremonies, cultural programs, and various side events, showcasing the diverse heritage and artistic talent of Paris.

Additionally, community organizations are involved in volunteer recruitment and training, ensuring that local knowledge and enthusiasm are harnessed to enhance the visitor experience. These partnerships help foster a sense of ownership and pride among Parisians, making the Games a true celebration of the city and its people.

Educational Institutions and Youth Engagement

Paris 2024 places a strong emphasis on engaging young people and educational institutions. Schools, colleges, and universities across.

France are participating in Olympic-related programs, promoting the values of sportsmanship, teamwork, and healthy living. Educational initiatives include Olympic-themed curricula, sports clinics, and cultural exchange programs, all designed to inspire the next generation of athletes and global citizens.

The Youth Olympic Games, a companion event to the main Olympics, further emphasizes this focus. Young athletes from around the world come together to compete, learn, and share their cultures, creating a vibrant and dynamic atmosphere that complements the traditional Olympic Games.

Funding and Financial Management

Hosting the Olympics requires meticulous financial planning and management. The costs involved are substantial, covering everything from venue construction and upgrades to security, transportation, and hospitality. Paris 2024 has developed a comprehensive financial plan to ensure that the Games are well-funded and managed efficiently.

Budget and Financial Planning

The budget for the 2024 Paris Olympics is estimated to be several billion euros. This budget is carefully allocated to cover various aspects of the Games, including infrastructure, operations, marketing, and legacy projects. Financial planning involves detailed forecasting and contingency planning to account for potential risks and uncertainties.

Revenue Sources

The primary sources of revenue for the Olympics include:

- **Sponsorships:** As discussed earlier, sponsorship deals with global and local partners provide significant financial support.

- **Broadcasting Rights:** The sale of broadcasting rights to television networks and digital platforms generates substantial revenue. The global reach of the Olympics makes these rights highly valuable.

- **Ticket Sales:** Revenue from ticket sales for events, ceremonies, and other Olympic-related activities is another major source of income. Paris 2024 aims to make tickets accessible to a wide audience, balancing affordability with revenue goals.

- **Merchandising:** Official Olympic merchandise, ranging from apparel and accessories to memorabilia, contributes to the overall revenue. These products allow fans to show their support and take home a piece of the Olympic spirit.

- **Public Funding:** The French government and local authorities provide financial support, particularly for infrastructure projects and public services related to the Games.

Cost Management and Efficiency

Efficient cost management is crucial to ensuring that the Olympics stay within budget and deliver value for money. Paris 2024 has adopted several strategies to achieve this:

- **Use of Existing Venues:** By utilizing existing sports facilities and venues, Paris 2024 minimizes the need for new construction, reducing costs and environmental impact.

- **Sustainable Practices:** Implementing sustainable practices not only aligns with environmental goals but also helps reduce operational costs. This includes energy-efficient infrastructure, waste reduction, and sustainable transportation options.

- **Public-Private Partnerships:** Collaborating with private sector partners for funding and operational support allows for cost-sharing and reduces the financial burden on public resources.

Legacy and Long-Term Impact

One of the most important considerations for any Olympic Games is the legacy it leaves behind. Paris 2024 is committed to ensuring that the Games have a positive and lasting impact on the city, the country, and the global community.

Here are some of the long term impacts to expect:

Urban Development and Infrastructure

The infrastructure improvements made for the Olympics will benefit Paris long after the Games have concluded. Upgrades to public transportation, road networks, and sports facilities will enhance the quality of life for residents and visitors. The Olympic Village, for example, will be repurposed into housing and community spaces, providing a lasting benefit to the local population.

Economic Boost

Hosting the Olympics has a tremendous economic impact.

The influx of tourists, increased global visibility, and investments in infrastructure stimulate economic growth. Local businesses, from hotels and restaurants to retail stores and service providers, benefit from the increased activity and international attention.

Social and Cultural Impact

The Olympics provide an opportunity to promote social cohesion and cultural exchange. Community engagement initiatives, educational programs, and cultural events foster a sense of unity and pride among residents. The emphasis on inclusivity and diversity ensures that the Games reflect and celebrate the rich cultural heritage of Paris and its people.

Environmental Sustainability

Paris 2024 is dedicated to setting new standards for environmental sustainability in major sporting events. By prioritizing eco-friendly practices and minimizing the environmental footprint, the organizers aim to create a model for future Olympic Games. The sustainability initiatives implemented for the 2024 Olympics will leave a lasting legacy, promoting environmental awareness and action in Paris and beyond.

Conclusion

The organizational structure behind the 2024 Paris Olympics is a complex and dynamic system involving multiple stakeholders, from the International Olympic Committee to local volunteers. Each element, from sponsorships and partnerships to volunteer involvement and financial management, plays a crucial role in bringing the Games to life.

As we look forward to the 2024 Olympics, it's clear that the efforts of these dedicated organizations and individuals will result in an event that not only showcases the pinnacle of athletic achievement but also celebrates the spirit of Paris and its people. The legacy of the Games will be felt for years to come, leaving a positive and lasting impact on the city, the country, and the global community.

So, whether you're a spectator, a volunteer, or simply a fan of the Olympics, take a moment to appreciate the incredible effort and collaboration that make this event possible. The 2024 Paris

Olympics is going to be an unforgettable celebration of sport, culture, and unity, so make sure you enjoy every bit of it.

CHAPTER THREE
Sports and Disciplines

This chapter highlights the heart and soul of the Olympic Games: the sports and disciplines that bring together athletes from around the globe in a celebration of skill, dedication, and competition. In this chapter, we'll explore the wide array of sports featured in the 2024 Paris Olympics, highlight some new and returning events, provide a detailed schedule of events, and guide you through the venue locations where all the action will unfold. It doesn't matter if you're a die-hard sports fan or a curious newcomer, there's something for everyone at the 2024 Olympics.

Overview of Olympic Sports

The Olympic Games are renowned for their diverse range of sports, showcasing everything from traditional track and field events to modern extreme sports. The 2024 Paris Olympics will feature 32 sports and 329 events, offering a platform for both seasoned Olympians and emerging talents to shine. Here's a quick overview of the main categories of Olympic sports you can look forward to:

Athletics

Athletics, often referred to as track and field, is one of the cornerstones of the Olympics. These events include running, jumping, and throwing disciplines, and they take place at the iconic Stade de France. From the lightning-fast 100-meter dash to the grueling marathon, athletics tests the limits of human speed, endurance, and skill.

Aquatics

Aquatics encompasses swimming, diving, water polo, and artistic swimming. These events are held at the Paris Aquatics Centre and other venues. Swimming features a variety of strokes and distances, while diving showcases athletes' acrobatic skills. Artistic swimming, formerly known as synchronized swimming, combines grace and precision, and water polo offers intense team competition in the pool.

Gymnastics

Gymnastics includes artistic, rhythmic, and trampoline disciplines. Artistic gymnastics, held at the Bercy Arena, features events like the vault, balance beam, and parallel bars. Rhythmic gymnastics, also at Bercy Arena, combines dance and gymnastics using ribbons, hoops, and balls. Trampoline gymnastics highlights athletes' aerial acrobatics and precision.

Team Sports

The Olympics feature a range of team sports, including basketball, football, volleyball, handball, and hockey. These sports are played at various venues across Paris, bringing together teams from around the world to compete for gold.

Team sports foster camaraderie, strategy, and teamwork, making them some of the most exciting events to watch.

Combat Sports

Combat sports include boxing, judo, taekwondo, and wrestling. These intense, one-on-one battles test athletes' strength, technique, and mental toughness. Combat sports are hosted at venues like the Paris Expo Porte de Versailles and showcase the spirit of martial arts and combat disciplines.

Racket Sports

Racket sports such as tennis, table tennis, and badminton are always fan favorites. Tennis events take place at the historic Roland Garros, while table tennis and badminton are held at the Paris Expo Porte de Versailles. These sports require agility, precision, and strategic thinking, making for thrilling matches.

Cycling

Cycling is a multifaceted sport at the Olympics, including road cycling, track cycling, mountain biking, and BMX. Events are held at various venues, including the Velodrome de Saint-Quentin-en-Yvelines and scenic locations across Paris. Cycling tests endurance, speed, and technical skills, offering a variety of thrilling races.

Equestrian

Equestrian events, held at the stunning Palace of Versailles, include dressage, show jumping, and eventing. These disciplines showcase the incredible bond between horse and rider, highlighting precision, agility, and mutual trust.

Extreme and New Sports

The Olympics continue to evolve, and the 2024 Games will feature several extreme and new sports. Skateboarding, sport climbing, and surfing are among the exciting additions. These sports appeal to younger audiences and bring fresh energy to the Games.

New and Returning Sports

The Olympic Games are constantly evolving to reflect changing interests and trends in sports. The 2024 Paris Olympics will see the return of some fan-favorite sports and the introduction of exciting new disciplines. Let's take a closer look at what's new and what's making a comeback.

New Sports

1. Breaking (Breakdancing)

One of the most anticipated new additions to the 2024 Olympics is breaking, also known as breakdancing. This dynamic and expressive street dance style will make its Olympic debut in Paris, reflecting the growing popularity of urban sports. Breaking competitions will feature "battles" where dancers showcase their skills, creativity, and athleticism in head-to-head matchups.

2. Skateboarding

Skateboarding made its Olympic debut in Tokyo 2020 and is back for Paris 2024. The sport includes two disciplines: street and park. Street skateboarding takes place on a course with stairs, rails, and other urban obstacles, while park skateboarding features a bowl-like course with ramps and curves. Skateboarding brings a youthful, vibrant energy to the Olympics and is sure to captivate audiences.

3. Surfing

Surfing also debuted in Tokyo 2020 and returns for the Paris Games, although the surfing events will take place in Tahiti, French Polynesia, known for its world-class waves. Surfers will compete in various wave conditions, demonstrating their skill and adaptability. The inclusion of surfing highlights the global nature of the Olympics and the diversity of sports.

4. Sport Climbing

Sport climbing, another newcomer from Tokyo 2020, will be featured again in Paris. This sport includes three disciplines:

lead climbing, speed climbing, and bouldering. Athletes will showcase their strength, agility, and problem-solving skills as they scale challenging routes on artificial climbing walls.

Returning Sports

1. Baseball/Softball

Baseball and softball made a return to the Olympics in Tokyo after being absent since 2008, and they are back for Paris 2024. These sports are incredibly popular in many parts of the world and bring a team-oriented dynamic to the Games. Baseball and softball events will be held at dedicated venues, offering exciting games and showcasing the sport's unique appeal.

2. Karate

Karate made its Olympic debut in Tokyo and will return for Paris 2024. This traditional martial art focuses on kata (forms) and kumite (sparring), highlighting both the technical and combat aspects of the discipline. Karate's inclusion in the Olympics underscores the importance of martial arts and their cultural significance.

3. 3x3 Basketball

3x3 basketball, a fast-paced and entertaining variation on traditional basketball, returns following a successful premiere in Tokyo.

Played on a half-court with three players on each team, 3x3 basketball is known for its quick gameplay and high-scoring action. This sport appeals to both basketball enthusiasts and casual fans alike.

Schedule of Events

The Olympic schedule is a meticulously planned and carefully coordinated timeline that ensures every sport and event is given its moment in the spotlight. The 2024 Paris Olympics will run from July 26 to August 11, offering 17 days of nonstop action. Here's a day-by-day breakdown of the key events and highlights:

Day 1: July 26

- Opening Ceremony at Stade de France

Day 2: July 27

- Swimming preliminaries and finals at Paris Aquatic Centre

- Men's and women's road cycling race starting at the Eiffel Tower and finishing on the Champs-Élysées

- Men's and women's gymnastics qualifications at Bercy Arena

Day 3: July 28

- Athletics competitions begin at Stade de France, including the men's 100m heats

- Women's beach volleyball preliminary matches at Champ de Mars

- Men's basketball group stage games at Bercy Arena

Day 4: July 29

- Women's artistic gymnastics team finals at Bercy Arena

- Men's and women's swimming finals at Paris Aquatics Centre

- Equestrian dressage at the Palace of Versailles

Day 5: July 30

- Men's artistic gymnastics team finals at Bercy Arena

- Men's and women's weightlifting finals at Palais des Sports

- Women's football quarterfinals at Parc des Princes

Day 6: July 31

- Men's and women's triathlon at Pont Alexandre III

- Men's and women's rowing finals at Vaires-sur-Marne Nautical Stadium

- Men's basketball quarterfinals at Bercy Arena

Day 7: August 1

- Women's 100m final at Stade de France

- Men's and women's tennis finals to be hosted at Roland Garros

- Men's handball quarterfinals at Paris Expo Porte de Versailles

Day 8: August

- Men's 100m final at Stade de France

- Men's and women's BMX finals at BMX Stadium, Saint-Quentin-en-Yvelines

- Women's basketball semifinals at Bercy Arena

Day 9: August 3

- Women's heptathlon final events at Stade de France

- Men's and women's judo finals at Paris Expo Porte de Versailles

- Men's football semifinals at Parc des Princes

Day 10: August 4

- Men's decathlon final events at Stade de France

- Men's and women's badminton finals at Paris Expo Porte de Versailles

- Women's water polo final at Paris Aquatics Centre

Day 11: August 5

- Women's marathon starting at Hôtel de Ville and ending at Champs-Élysées

- Men's and women's sport climbing finals at Le Bourget Climbing Centre

- Men's basketball semifinals at Bercy Arena

Day 12: August 6

- Men's marathon starting at Hôtel de Ville and ending at Champs-Élysées

- Men's and women's wrestling finals at Paris Expo Porte de Versailles

- Men's and women's table tennis finals at Paris Expo Porte de Versailles

Day 13: August 7

- Men's and women's diving finals at Paris Aquatics Centre

- Men's football final at Stade de France

- Women's volleyball final at Paris Expo Porte de Versailles

Day 14: August 8

- Men's and women's skateboarding finals at Place de la Concorde

- Men's handball final at Paris Expo Porte de Versailles

- Women's basketball final at Bercy Arena

Day 15: August 9

- Men's and women's rhythmic gymnastics finals at Bercy Arena

- Men's volleyball final at Paris Expo Porte de Versailles

- Women's football final at Parc des Princes

Day 16: August 10

- Men's 4x100m relay final at Stade de France

- Women's 4x100m relay final at Stade de France

- Men's water polo final at Paris Aquatics Centre

Day 17: August 11

- Men's and women's 4x400m relay finals at Stade de France

- Men's basketball final at Bercy Arena

- Closing Ceremony at Stade de France

Venue Locations for Each Sport

The Paris 2024 Olympics will take advantage of some of the city's most iconic locations as well as purpose-built venues to host the wide array of sports. Here's a detailed guide to where you can catch all the action:

Stade de France

- Athletics
- Opening and Closing Ceremonies
- Football finals

Paris Aquatics Centre

- Swimming
- Diving
- Water polo

- Artistic swimming

Bercy Arena (AccorHotels Arena)

- Artistic gymnastics
- Rhythmic gymnastics
- Trampoline gymnastics
- Basketball

Roland Garros

- Tennis

Parc des Princes

- Football

Champ de Mars

- Beach volleyball

Grand Palais

- Fencing

Palais des Sports

- Weightlifting

Palace of Versailles

- Equestrian (dressage, show jumping, eventing)

Velodrome de Saint-Quentin-en-Yvelines

- Track cycling

Le Bourget Climbing Centre

- Sport climbing

Place de la Concorde

- Skateboarding

Paris Expo Porte de Versailles

- Handball
- Table tennis
- Badminton
- Judo
- Wrestling
- Taekwondo

BMX Stadium, Saint-Quentin-en-Yvelines

- BMX cycling

Vaires-sur-Marne Nautical Stadium

- Rowing
- Canoe sprint

Pont Alexandre III

- Triathlon

Hôtel de Ville

- Marathon start and finish

Champs-Élysées

- Road cycling finish
- Marathon finish

Place de la Concorde

- Breaking (Breakdancing)

Final Thoughts

The 2024 Paris Olympics promise to be an extraordinary display of athletic excellence, cultural joy, and worldwide solidarity.

Whether you're attending in person, watching from home, or following your favorite events online, you'll be part of a global community united by the love of sport. The venues spread across Paris will not only host incredible competitions but also provide stunning backdrops that highlight the city's beauty and history.

As you plan your Olympic experience, use this guide to navigate the schedule, discover the venues, and learn about the sports that will captivate audiences around the world. The 2024 Paris Olympics are more than just a series of competitions; they are a testament to human achievement, a celebration of diversity, and a showcase of the enduring Olympic spirit.

We hope you enjoy every moment of this extraordinary event, and may the Games inspire you to strive for excellence, embrace friendship, and show respect for all.

CHAPTER FOUR
Athletes to Watch

This is one of the most exciting chapters of our book: the athletes who will be making headlines, breaking records, and inspiring millions at the 2024 Paris Olympics. This chapter is all about the stars of the show—the top contenders, rising talents, and legendary Olympians who embody the spirit of the Games. We'll also explore the diversity and inclusivity that enrich the athlete pool, ensuring that the 2024 Olympics are a true reflection of our global community.

Profiles of Top Contenders

Every Olympic Games has its standout athletes—those who have consistently proven their mettle and are poised to achieve greatness. Here are some of the top contenders you'll want to keep an eye on during the 2024 Paris Olympics:

1. Simone Biles (USA) – Gymnastics

Simone Biles needs no introduction. Widely regarded as the greatest gymnast of all time, Biles has already secured her place in history with her incredible performances in Rio 2016 and Tokyo 2020. Known for her powerful routines and groundbreaking skills, she holds multiple world championship titles and Olympic gold medals. At Paris 2024, Biles will be aiming to further cement her legacy, and you won't want to miss her breathtaking routines.

2. Eliud Kipchoge (Kenya) – Marathon

Eliud Kipchoge, the marathon world record holder, is a true legend in long-distance running. With gold medals from Rio 2016 and Tokyo 2020, Kipchoge is the favorite to defend his title in Paris. Known for his calm demeanor and unmatched endurance, he made history by running a marathon in under two hours, albeit in a non-competitive event. Watch for Kipchoge to potentially achieve another historic victory on the streets of Paris.

3. Katie Ledecky (USA) – Swimming

Katie Ledecky has been a dominant force in women's swimming since her breakout performance at the 2012 London Olympics. With multiple Olympic gold medals and world records to her name, Ledecky is renowned for her incredible stamina and speed in distance freestyle events. In Paris, she will likely compete in several events, adding to her already impressive medal tally and possibly setting new records.

4. Armand Duplantis (Sweden) – Pole Vault

Armand "Mondo" Duplantis holds the current pole vault world record and is a favorite to win gold in Paris. With his remarkable technique and consistent performances, Duplantis has revolutionized the sport, breaking records both indoors and outdoors. At just 24 years old, he has already achieved more than many athletes do in a lifetime, and he is poised to add an Olympic gold to his accolades in 2024.

5. Shelly-Ann Fraser-Pryce (Jamaica) – Athletics

Shelly-Ann Fraser-Pryce, often dubbed the "Pocket Rocket," is one of the fastest women in history. With multiple Olympic golds in the 100m, she has consistently dominated the sprinting world. Even in her mid-30s, Fraser-Pryce continues to perform at an elite level, making her a strong contender for more medals in Paris. Her rivalry with other top sprinters promises thrilling races.

6. Neeraj Chopra (India) – Javelin Throw

Neeraj Chopra made history by winning India's first-ever Olympic gold medal in track and field at the Tokyo 2020 Games. As a javelin thrower, Chopra has consistently pushed the boundaries, setting national and continental records. His victory has ignited a surge of interest in athletics in India, and he is expected to be a strong contender for another gold in Paris 2024.

7. Naomi Osaka (Japan) – Tennis

Naomi Osaka, a four-time Grand Slam champion, has become a global icon both on and off the court. Known for her powerful serve and baseline play, Osaka is a fierce competitor who has already left her mark on the sport. Beyond her athletic prowess, she is also celebrated for her activism and advocacy for mental health awareness. In Paris, she will be looking to add an Olympic medal to her impressive collection.

8. Katarina Johnson-Thompson (Great Britain) – Heptathlon

Katarina Johnson-Thompson is one of the most versatile athletes in track and field. Specializing in the heptathlon, she combines speed, strength, and agility across seven events. After overcoming injuries, Johnson-Thompson is poised for a strong comeback in Paris, where she hopes to challenge for the gold medal and solidify her status as one of the best multi-event athletes in the world.

9. Karsten Warholm (Norway) – Athletics

Karsten Warholm set the track world on fire with his record-breaking performance in the 400 meters hurdles at the Tokyo 2020 Olympics. His time of 45.94 seconds shattered the previous world record and secured him a gold medal. Warholm's intense training regimen and relentless drive make him a top contender to defend his title in Paris 2024.

10. Tadej Pogačar (Slovenia) – Cycling

Tadej Pogačar has quickly established himself as one of the top cyclists in the world, winning the Tour de France in 2020 and 2021. His climbing prowess and tactical acumen have made him a force to be reckoned with in both stage races and one-day classics. Pogačar will be aiming for Olympic glory in the road cycling events in Paris.

11. Dina Asher-Smith (Great Britain) – Athletics

Dina Asher-Smith is Britain's fastest woman and a medal contender in the sprints. With a World Championship title in the 200 meters and multiple European titles, Asher-Smith has proven her speed and consistency. In Paris, she will be looking to add Olympic medals to her collection, competing in both the 100 meters and 200 meters.

Rising Stars and Newcomers

The Olympics are also a stage for emerging talents—young athletes who are set to become the next big names in their sports. Let's meet some of the rising stars and newcomers who could steal the spotlight in Paris.

1. Sky Brown (Great Britain) – Skateboarding

Sky Brown made history in Tokyo 2020 as Great Britain's youngest ever Olympian, winning a bronze medal in skateboarding at just 13 years old. With her fearless style and infectious enthusiasm, Brown is a star in the making. In Paris, she will be a strong contender for gold, and her performances are sure to inspire a new generation of skateboarders.

2. Erriyon Knighton (USA) – Athletics

At just 18 years old, Erriyon Knighton is already being compared to Usain Bolt. The American sprinter has broken Bolt's U20 records in the 200m and is rapidly making a name for himself on the senior circuit. With his incredible speed and potential, Knighton is a rising star to watch, and he could very well be the next great sprinter to dominate the Olympics.

3. Momiji Nishiya (Japan) – Skateboarding

Momiji Nishiya won gold in the inaugural women's street skateboarding event in Tokyo 2020 at just 13 years old. Her smooth style and technical prowess have quickly made her one of the sport's brightest stars. Nishiya will be looking to defend her title in Paris and continue her ascent in the skateboarding world.

4. Carlos Yulo (Philippines) – Gymnastics

Carlos Yulo has been making waves in gymnastics with his impressive performances on the world stage. Specializing in floor exercise and vault, Yulo became the first Filipino gymnast to win a world championship title. His dynamic routines and high difficulty levels make him a strong medal contender in Paris.

5. Leylah Fernandez (Canada) – Tennis

Leylah Fernandez burst onto the scene with her incredible run to the final of the 2021 US Open. Known for her tenacity and powerful baseline play, Fernandez has quickly become one of the most exciting young talents in tennis. In Paris, she will be looking to make her mark and possibly secure an Olympic medal.

6. *Athing Mu (USA) – Athletics*

Athing Mu burst onto the scene with a dominant performance in the 800 meters at the Tokyo 2020 Olympics, winning gold at just 19 years old. Her smooth stride and tactical racing have made her one of the most promising young middle-distance runners. In Paris, Mu will aim to defend her title and perhaps even expand her range to other distances.

7. *Florian Wellbrock (Germany) – Swimming*

Florian Wellbrock is a rising star in the world of swimming, excelling in both the pool and open water. He won gold in the 10km open water swim and bronze in the 1500m freestyle at Tokyo 2020. Wellbrock's versatility and endurance make him a formidable competitor in multiple events, and he is expected to be a dominant force in Paris.

8. *Faith Kipyegon (Kenya) – Athletics*

Faith Kipyegon, the reigning Olympic champion in the 1500 meters, has consistently showcased her dominance in middle-distance running. Her tactical brilliance and finishing speed have earned her numerous titles and records. As she prepares for Paris 2024, Kipyegon remains a favorite to defend her title and possibly break more records.

9. Adriana Cerezo (Spain) – Taekwondo

Adriana Cerezo, at just 17 years old, won a silver medal in taekwondo at the Tokyo 2020 Olympics. Her impressive performance against seasoned competitors showcased her talent and potential. Cerezo is expected to continue her rise in the sport and could be a gold medal contender in Paris 2024.

10. Jackie Joyner-Kersee (USA) – Athletics

Jackie Joyner-Kersee is one of the most versatile and accomplished athletes in Olympic history, with six medals (three gold, one silver, two bronze) in the heptathlon and long jump. Her extraordinary performances and longevity in the sport have made her a role model for athletes worldwide. Joyner-Kersee's dedication and achievements continue to inspire new generations of track and field athletes.

11. Hicham El Guerrouj (Morocco) – Athletics

Hicham El Guerrouj is widely recognized as one of the most outstanding middle-distance runners of all time.

He won gold medals in the 1500 meters and 5000 meters at the Athens 2004 Olympics, a rare double that solidified his legacy. El Guerrouj holds world records in the 1500 meters, mile, and

2000 meters, and his dominance in the late 1990s and early 2000s remains unmatched.

Diversity and Inclusion in the Athlete Pool

The Olympic Games are a global celebration of humanity, bringing together athletes from diverse backgrounds and cultures. The 2024 Paris Olympics will continue to highlight the importance of diversity and inclusion, showcasing the rich tapestry of talent that makes the Games truly special.

Gender Equality

The Paris 2024 Olympics will be the most gender-balanced in history, with an equal number of events for men and women. This commitment to gender equality is a significant step forward for the Olympic Movement, ensuring that female athletes have the same opportunities to compete and excel as their male counterparts. From track and field to gymnastics, every sport will feature the incredible talents of women athletes, inspiring future generations.

Representation from All Continents

The Olympics provide a platform for athletes from every corner of the globe to compete on the world stage. The 2024 Games will feature participants from all continents, reflecting the universal appeal of sports. This diversity not only enriches the competition but also fosters greater understanding and unity among nations. Athletes from countries with smaller delegations will have the opportunity to showcase their skills and bring pride to their nations.

Inclusivity in New Sports

The inclusion of new and extreme sports in the Olympics has broadened the athlete pool, bringing in competitors from diverse backgrounds. Sports like skateboarding, surfing, and sport climbing attract young athletes from urban and rural areas alike, promoting inclusivity and expanding the reach of the Olympic Movement. These sports often emphasize creativity and individuality, providing a fresh perspective on athletic competition.

Refugee Olympic Team

The Refugee Olympic Team, first introduced in Rio 2016, will once again compete in Paris 2024. This team consists of athletes who have been displaced from their home countries due to conflict, persecution, or other crises. The inclusion of the Refugee Olympic Team highlights the resilience and determination of these athletes and raises awareness about the global refugee crisis. It also embodies the Olympic values of solidarity and peace.

Gender Identity and Participation

Discussions around gender identity and participation in sports have gained prominence in recent years. The IOC has updated its guidelines to promote fair and inclusive participation for transgender athletes. These guidelines emphasize the importance of respecting athletes' gender identities while ensuring fair competition. Paris 2024 will continue to navigate these complex issues, striving to create an environment where all athletes can compete authentically and safely.

Athletes from Underrepresented Communities

Efforts to support and develop talent in underrepresented communities have led to greater diversity in the athlete pool. Initiatives by national and international sports organizations aim to identify and nurture talent in regions with less access to resources and training facilities. These efforts ensure that athletes from all backgrounds have the opportunity to compete at the highest level. Programs such as scholarships, grassroots development, and community outreach are helping to level the playing field, bringing new and diverse talents to the fore.

CHAPTER FIVE
Opening and Closing Ceremonies

This chapter examines the grand stages of the 2024 Paris Olympics—the opening and closing ceremonies. These ceremonies are not just events; they are the heartbeats of the Games, setting the tone for the athletic competition to come and celebrating the accomplishments once it concludes. In this chapter, we will explore the themes and highlights of the opening ceremony, key performances and moments, and the cultural significance and symbolism embedded in these spectacular displays. Let's dive into the magic and pageantry that will bookend the 2024 Olympic Games.

Themes and Highlights of the Opening Ceremony

The opening ceremony is where the world gets its first glimpse of the host city's unique flair and cultural richness. For Paris 2024, the ceremony promises to be a blend of tradition, innovation, and a celebration of humanity's resilience and unity.

1. Celebrating Parisian Heritage:

Paris, known as "The City of Light," will shine brightly in the opening ceremony, celebrating its rich history and cultural heritage. Expect a spectacular showcase of Parisian landmarks, art, and fashion. The Eiffel Tower, the Louvre, and the Seine

River will serve as stunning backdrops, integrating the city's iconic elements into the ceremony.

2. *Unity and Inclusivity:*

A major theme of the 2024 Olympics is unity and inclusivity. The opening ceremony will emphasize the spirit of togetherness, bringing people from diverse backgrounds together through the universal language of sport. This theme will be reflected in the choreography, music, and narratives that highlight the importance of peace, solidarity, and mutual respect.

3. *Environmental Sustainability:*

In line with the commitment to sustainability, the Paris 2024 opening ceremony will also focus on environmental consciousness. Expect to see innovative use of renewable energy, eco-friendly materials, and messages promoting environmental stewardship. This emphasis on sustainability not only aligns with global priorities but also showcases Paris's leadership in green initiatives.

4. *Technological Innovation:*

Paris is at the forefront of technological advancements, and the opening ceremony will incorporate state-of-the-art technology to create an immersive experience. From augmented reality and drones to interactive light shows, technology will play a significant role in enhancing the visual and auditory spectacle of the ceremony.

5. Artistic Expression:

France is renowned for its artistic legacy, and the opening ceremony will pay homage to this heritage. Renowned artists, musicians, and performers will take center stage, blending traditional and contemporary forms of art. This celebration of creativity will highlight France's influence on global culture.

Key Performances and Moments

The opening ceremony of the Olympics is always filled with memorable performances and moments that capture the essence of the host city and the spirit of the Games. Here's a closer look at some of the key performances and moments you can expect at the Paris 2024 opening ceremony.

1. Aerial Spectacle over the Seine:

Imagine the Seine River transformed into a stage for a breathtaking aerial show. Using drones and light projections, the ceremony will feature an aerial ballet, showcasing the fluidity and grace of movement. This spectacle will highlight Paris's architectural beauty and its seamless integration with nature.

2. Parade of Nations:

The Parade of Nations is a time-honored tradition where athletes from around the world march into the stadium, proudly carrying their national flags. For Paris 2024, the parade will be especially meaningful, symbolizing the global unity and diversity that the Olympics represent. Each country's delegation will be welcomed with cheers and celebrations, highlighting the inclusivity of the Games.

3. Lighting of the Olympic Cauldron:

One of the most anticipated moments of the opening ceremony is the lighting of the Olympic cauldron. This ritual signifies the start of the Games and is always a closely guarded secret. In Paris, expect a dramatic and symbolic lighting that reflects the city's innovation and heritage. The cauldron's design and the journey of the Olympic flame through the city will be memorable highlights.

4. Musical Performances:

Music will be a central element of the ceremony, featuring performances by some of France's most celebrated artists. From classical compositions to contemporary hits, the musical journey will reflect the country's rich musical heritage. Special performances by international artists will also symbolize the global nature of the Games.

5. Artistic Displays and Dance:

France's love for ballet, modern dance, and theater will be on full display. Choreographed by leading artists, these performances will blend storytelling with intricate dance routines, creating visually stunning tableaux. Themes of peace, unity, and hope will be woven into these artistic displays, resonating with the global audience.

6. Messages of Peace and Solidarity:

As part of the ceremony, there will be poignant moments dedicated to messages of peace and solidarity. Speeches by notable figures, moments of silence for global challenges, and symbolic acts of unity will be incorporated to remind us of the Olympics' role in promoting peace and understanding among nations.

Cultural Significance and Symbolism

The opening ceremony is more than just a spectacle; it is imbued with deep cultural significance and symbolism. For Paris 2024, these elements will be meticulously crafted to reflect the city's identity and the values of the Olympic Movement.

1. The Eiffel Tower as a Beacon of Hope:

The Eiffel Tower, an enduring symbol of Paris, will be prominently featured in the opening ceremony. As a beacon of hope and resilience, the tower will be illuminated in dazzling lights, symbolizing the city's enduring spirit and its role as a host to the world. This iconic structure will serve as a reminder of the beauty and strength that Paris embodies.

2. The Olympic Rings and the Seine:

The Olympic rings are a powerful symbol of unity and the five continents coming together. For the opening ceremony, expect to see the rings creatively incorporated into the Seine River, perhaps through floating installations or light projections. This representation will highlight the connection between the Games and the city, emphasizing the inclusivity and harmony the rings symbolize.

3. Historical References:

Paris's rich history will be referenced throughout the ceremony, from its ancient roots to its role in shaping modern culture. Historical reenactments, visual projections, and artistic performances will transport the audience through time, showcasing the city's evolution and its contributions to the world.

4. Multicultural Celebrations:

As a cosmopolitan city, Paris is home to diverse cultures and communities. The opening ceremony will celebrate this multiculturalism through performances and segments representing various cultural heritages. This celebration will underscore the city's inclusivity and the harmonious coexistence of different cultures within its bounds.

5. Tributes to French Icons:

Expect tributes to iconic French figures who have left an indelible mark on the world. From literary giants like Victor Hugo to fashion icons like Coco Chanel, these tributes will honor the contributions of French luminaries to global culture. Their legacies will be highlighted through artistic interpretations and storytelling.

6. Symbolism of the Olympic Flame:

The journey of the Olympic flame, which culminates in the lighting of the cauldron, is rich in symbolism. Representing purity, peace, and the enduring spirit of competition, the flame's path through Paris will include significant landmarks, each chosen for its historical and cultural importance. This journey will symbolize the connection between the past, present, and future of the Olympic Movement.

The Closing Ceremony

While the opening ceremony sets the stage for the Games, the closing ceremony is a celebration of the achievements and spirit displayed throughout the competition. It is a moment of reflection, celebration, and farewell until the next gathering of the world's athletes. Let's explore the themes, key moments, and cultural significance of the closing ceremony for Paris 2024.

1. Celebrating Achievements:

The closing ceremony will honor the athletes' accomplishments, highlighting the stories of triumph, perseverance, and sportsmanship that have unfolded over the weeks. Medalists and participants will be celebrated, with special segments dedicated to their remarkable journeys and achievements.

2. Parisian Farewell:

As the host city, Paris will bid farewell to the world in a manner that reflects its elegance and charm. The ceremony will feature Parisian themes, including references to its art, fashion, and culinary delights. This farewell will be both a celebration of the city's role as a gracious host and an invitation for future visits.

3. Handing Over the Olympic Flag:

A significant moment in the closing ceremony is the handing over of the Olympic flag to the next host city. This symbolic act signifies the continuity of the Olympic Movement and the passing of responsibilities. The mayor of Paris will hand the flag to the representative of Los Angeles, the host city for the 2028 Olympics, accompanied by a short cultural showcase from the future hosts.

4. Performances and Entertainment:

Just like the opening ceremony, the closing ceremony will feature a variety of performances. Expect musical acts, dance performances, and artistic displays that encapsulate the spirit of the Games and the host city. These performances will serve as a celebration of global culture and unity.

5. Final Parade of Athletes:

The final parade of athletes is a more relaxed and joyous occasion compared to the formal parade during the opening ceremony. Athletes from all participating nations will march together, symbolizing the camaraderie and friendships formed during the Games. This parade is a visual representation of the unity and solidarity fostered by the Olympics.

6. Extinguishing the Olympic Flame:

The extinguishing of the Olympic flame marks the end of the Games. This poignant moment is filled with symbolism, signifying the conclusion of the event while also passing the spirit of the Games to the next host. The flame's final moments will be accompanied by reflective music and imagery, leaving a lasting impression on all who witness it.

Cultural Significance and Symbolism in the Closing Ceremony

The closing ceremony, like the opening, is rich in cultural significance and symbolism. It reflects the host city's pride in its successful hosting and the broader messages of the Olympic Movement.

1. Reflection and Farewell:

The closing ceremony provides an opportunity for reflection on the Games' impact and the shared experiences of athletes, spectators, and hosts. It is a moment to appreciate the collective effort that made the Games possible and to bid farewell until the next Olympic gathering.

2. Unity and Global Peace:

The theme of unity and global peace will be a central message in the closing ceremony. The visual and performing arts will convey the Olympic ideals of bringing people together through sport, transcending differences, and fostering mutual understanding. This message will be reinforced through the shared celebration of athletes from diverse nations marching together in the final parade.

3. Legacy of the Games:

The closing ceremony will also highlight the legacy of the Paris 2024 Olympics. This includes not only the physical infrastructure and improvements made in the city but also the lasting social and cultural impacts. Speeches and presentations will underscore how the Games have contributed to the local community and inspired future generations.

4. Symbolism of the Olympic Flame:

The extinguishing of the Olympic flame is a deeply symbolic act that marks the end of the current Games while keeping the spirit alive for the future. The flame's journey, which started with its lighting in Olympia and traveled through Paris, will be commemorated. This act symbolizes the continuity of the Olympic tradition and the enduring spirit of competition and friendship.

5. Cultural Showcase:

As part of the farewell, Paris will offer a cultural showcase that encapsulates the essence of French culture. This may include performances by renowned French artists, displays of French culinary art, and segments highlighting Paris's contributions to fashion, art, and philosophy. This cultural segment will be a final salute to the world, celebrating the host city's unique identity.

6. Handing Over to Los Angeles:

The handing over of the Olympic flag to Los Angeles will be a significant moment, symbolizing the continuity of the Olympic spirit. Los Angeles will provide a glimpse into what to expect in 2028, with a short cultural performance that introduces its own unique flavor and excitement. This moment connects the past, present, and future of the Olympic Games, maintaining the momentum and anticipation.

Key Performances and Moments in the Closing Ceremony

The closing ceremony, like the opening, will be filled with memorable performances and moments that capture the essence of the Games and the spirit of the host city. Here are a few highlights you can anticipate:

1. Musical Extravaganza:

Music will play a central role in the closing ceremony, featuring a mix of traditional French tunes and contemporary hits. Renowned French musicians, as well as international artists, will take the stage, creating a festive and celebratory atmosphere. Expect collaborations that blend different genres and cultural influences, reflecting the global nature of the Games.

2. Dance and Artistic Displays:

Dance performances will highlight the closing ceremony, with intricate choreography that tells stories of unity, resilience, and joy. From classical ballet to modern dance, these performances will be visually stunning and emotionally resonant. Artistic displays, including light shows and projections, will enhance the visual spectacle, creating an immersive experience for viewers.

3. Athlete Celebrations:

The final parade of athletes is always a joyous occasion, where competitors from different nations come together in a spirit of camaraderie. This informal parade allows athletes to celebrate their achievements, forge new friendships, and reflect on their Olympic journey. It is a heartwarming display of the connections and shared experiences that define the Games.

4. Speeches and Reflections:

Speeches by key figures, including the IOC President and the Mayor of Paris, will reflect on the success and impact of the Games. These speeches will acknowledge the efforts of everyone involved, from athletes and coaches to volunteers and organizers. They will also highlight the importance of the Olympic values and the positive legacy the Games leave behind.

5. Extinguishing the Olympic Flame:

The extinguishing of the Olympic flame is a powerful and emotional moment. It signifies the end of the Games while symbolizing the enduring spirit that will continue until the next Olympics. This moment will be accompanied by reflective music and visuals, creating a poignant and memorable conclusion to the ceremony.

Final Thoughts

The opening and closing ceremonies of the 2024 Paris Olympics are more than just spectacles; they are powerful narratives that encapsulate the spirit of the Games, the essence of the host city, and the unity of the global community. Through themes of heritage, unity, sustainability, and innovation, these ceremonies will showcase the best of Paris and the Olympic Movement.

As you prepare to watch these ceremonies, whether in person or from afar, take a moment to appreciate the thought, creativity, and effort that go into making them unforgettable. These events are not just the bookends of the Olympic Games; they are celebrations of human potential, resilience, and the unbreakable bonds that sport can create.

CHAPTER SIX
Medal Events

In this chapter, we dig into the heart of the competition—the medal events. The thrill of victory and the agony of defeat come to life through the stories of athletes who reach the pinnacle of their sports. We will explore the medal tally and leaderboard, historic medal wins and records, a country-by-country breakdown, and inspirational stories of triumph that define the 2024 Paris Olympics. Let's embark on this journey of excellence and inspiration together.

Medal Tally and Leaderboard

The medal tally is a central focus during the Olympic Games, showcasing which countries and athletes are leading in the competition. It's a dynamic and thrilling aspect of the Games, reflecting the intense effort and dedication of the competitors.

1. Overview of the Medal Tally:

The medal tally provides a snapshot of the overall performance of each country, including the number of gold, silver, and bronze medals won. The tally is updated in real-time, keeping fans and athletes engaged throughout the Games. Here's how you can track the progress:

- ***Gold Medals:*** These are awarded to the first-place finishers in each event, representing the highest achievement.

- **Silver Medals:** Given to the second-place finishers, showcasing their remarkable efforts.

- **Bronze Medals:** Awarded to the third-place finishers, acknowledging their outstanding performance.

2. Leaderboard Dynamics:

The leaderboard often shifts dramatically as different events conclude. A strong performance in a single event can propel a country to the top, while consistent success across multiple events ensures a steady presence. Key sports like athletics, swimming, and gymnastics typically have a significant impact on the leaderboard due to the number of events they encompass.

Historic Medal Wins and Records

The Olympics are a stage where history is made, with athletes breaking records and achieving feats that become part of the Games' lore. Let's look at some historic medal wins and records that could shape the 2024 Paris Olympics.

1. Record-Breaking Performances:

Every Olympic Games features athletes who push the boundaries of what is possible. In Paris 2024, we anticipate seeing new world and Olympic records being set in various disciplines. Here are a few potential highlights:

- ***Track and Field:*** Athletes like Karsten Warholm in the 400 meters hurdles and Mondo Duplantis in the pole vault could set new world records, building on their incredible performances leading up to the Games.

- ***Swimming:*** Swimmers like Katie Ledecky and Caeleb Dressel have the potential to break multiple world records, given their track record of exceptional performances.

- ***Gymnastics:*** Simone Biles, with her groundbreaking routines, might achieve new records for the highest scores ever in gymnastics.

2. Historic Medal Wins:

Some medal wins go beyond the numbers and records; they resonate deeply due to their historic significance:

- ***Firsts for Countries:*** Watching a country win its first-ever Olympic medal is always a momentous occasion. For instance, athletes from countries with smaller delegations or less Olympic history might make headlines by clinching their nation's inaugural gold.

- ***Comebacks and Milestones:*** Athletes who make successful comebacks after injuries or long absences often provide some of the most inspiring stories. Their victories become milestones in Olympic history.

Country-by-Country Breakdown

The Olympics are a global event, and the medal tally reflects the diverse range of countries that excel in various sports. Here's a closer look at how some key countries are expected to perform at the Paris 2024 Olympics.

1. United States

The United States has historically been a dominant force in the Olympics, and Paris 2024 will likely be no different. With strengths in athletics, swimming, gymnastics, and team sports, the U.S. is expected to feature prominently on the leaderboard. Key athletes to watch include Simone Biles, Katie Ledecky, Caeleb Dressel, and the U.S. basketball teams.

2. China

China has emerged as a powerhouse in recent Olympic Games, particularly in sports like diving, gymnastics, table tennis, and weightlifting. Chinese athletes are known for their discipline and precision, often excelling in events requiring technical skill and consistency.

3. Russia

Competing under the ROC (Russian Olympic Committee) due to doping sanctions, Russian athletes remain formidable contenders in various sports, including gymnastics, wrestling, and fencing. Their performances are closely watched, and they often secure a significant number of medals.

4. Great Britain

Great Britain has seen a resurgence in its Olympic fortunes over the past few Games, excelling in cycling, rowing, athletics, and equestrian events. Athletes like Dina Asher-Smith and Adam Peaty are expected to lead the charge for Team GB in Paris.

5. Japan

As the host of the Tokyo 2020 Olympics, Japan showcased its strengths in judo, wrestling, gymnastics, and newly added sports like skateboarding. With the Games now moving to Paris, Japanese athletes will continue to aim for strong performances and build on their recent successes.

6. Australia

Australia is traditionally strong in swimming, field hockey, and cycling. Swimmers like Ariarne Titmus and Kyle Chalmers are expected to shine in Paris, adding to Australia's impressive Olympic legacy.

7. Germany

Germany excels in sports like equestrian, canoeing, rowing, and handball. German athletes are known for their meticulous preparation and strategic approach to competition, often leading to strong medal performances.

8. Kenya

Kenya's dominance in long-distance running is unparalleled, with athletes like Eliud Kipchoge leading the way. The country consistently produces world-class runners who excel in marathons and other distance events, making them a key contender in athletics.

Anticipated Medal Events at Paris 2024

With a myriad of events taking place, some medal events are particularly anticipated due to their history, the athletes involved, or the sheer excitement they generate. Here are some of the highlights you can look forward to:

1. Men's and Women's 100 Meters (Athletics)

The 100 meters is often dubbed the "fastest event in the world." The showdown to determine the fastest man and woman on earth is always a highlight. With athletes like Dina Asher-Smith and Shelly-Ann Fraser-Pryce in the women's event, and new talents emerging in the men's event, these races promise to be thrilling.

2. Gymnastics All-Around Competitions

The gymnastics all-around competitions are the ultimate tests of versatility and skill in the sport. Simone Biles, if she competes, will be a major draw, but the competition will be fierce with other top gymnasts from around the world showcasing their talents.

3. Men's and Women's Marathon

The marathon is a grueling test of endurance and strategy. Eliud Kipchoge, aiming for his third consecutive Olympic gold, will be the athlete to watch. On the women's side, the field is wide open with several strong contenders vying for the top spot.

4. Swimming Relay Events

The swimming relays—particularly the 4x100m and 4x200m freestyle relays—are always exciting, with teams vying for national pride and Olympic glory. The U.S. teams, traditionally strong in these events, will face stiff competition from Australia, Great Britain, and others.

5. Men's and Women's Basketball Finals

Basketball is a global sport, and the Olympic finals are a showcase of the best talent from around the world. The U.S. teams, perennial favorites, will face strong challenges from countries like Spain, France, and Australia.

6. Men's and Women's Cycling (Track and Road)

Cycling events, both track and road, are filled with intense competition and strategy. In the velodrome, watch for riders like Great Britain's Laura Kenny and the Netherlands' Harrie Lavreysen. On the road, the Tour de France champions like Tadej Pogačar will be aiming to add Olympic gold to their accolades.

7. Men's and Women's Diving

Diving combines athleticism with grace, making it one of the most visually captivating sports at the Olympics. China's diving team has historically dominated, but athletes from countries like the UK, Australia, and the USA will be challenging for the top spots.

8. Team Sports (Football, Volleyball, Field Hockey)

Team sports bring together not only the best players from around the world but also passionate fans. Football (soccer) tournaments, both men's and women's, will see countries like Brazil, Germany, and the USA battling for gold. In volleyball, teams from Brazil, the USA, and Russia are perennial powerhouses. Field hockey, especially with teams like the Netherlands, Australia, and India, will feature high-intensity matches.

9. Equestrian Events

Equestrian events, including dressage, eventing, and show jumping, showcase the unique partnership between rider and horse. Riders like Germany's Michael Jung and the UK's Charlotte Dujardin are expected to shine. The stunning backdrop of the Palace of Versailles will add to the spectacle.

10. New and Returning Sports

Paris 2024 will feature new sports and the return of popular ones. Breaking (breakdancing) will debut, showcasing incredible athleticism and creativity. Surfing, skateboarding, and sport climbing, which were introduced in Tokyo 2020, will return, attracting a younger audience and adding new dynamics to the Games.

Inspirational Stories of Triumph

Beyond the podium finishes and records, the Olympics are defined by the human stories of perseverance, dedication, and triumph. Here are some inspirational stories that exemplify the spirit of the Games:

1. Simone Biles – A Champion's Resilience

Simone Biles' decision to prioritize her mental health during the Tokyo 2020 Olympics was a powerful statement that resonated worldwide. Her return to competition in Paris, potentially achieving new heights, will be a testament to her resilience and strength. Biles' journey continues to inspire athletes to prioritize their well-being and speak openly about mental health.

2. Neeraj Chopra – Inspiring a Nation

Neeraj Chopra's historic gold medal in javelin throw at Tokyo 2020 not only put him in the global spotlight but also inspired a new generation of athletes in India. Chopra's humble beginnings and rise to Olympic champion illustrate the power of hard work and determination. His continued success in Paris will further ignite passion for athletics in his home country.

3. The Refugee Olympic Team – Symbol of Hope

The Refugee Olympic Team embodies hope and resilience. These athletes, displaced by conflict and adversity, represent the unbreakable spirit of those who have been forced to leave their homes. Their participation in the Olympics sends a powerful message of solidarity and the universal nature of sport.

4. Allyson Felix – Legacy of Excellence

Allyson Felix's remarkable career, marked by 11 Olympic medals and her advocacy for athlete mothers, continues to inspire. Her performance in Tokyo, after becoming a mother and overcoming numerous challenges, added to her legendary status. As she potentially competes in her final Olympics in

Paris, Felix's legacy will be celebrated by fans and fellow athletes alike.

5. Athing Mu – Rising Star

Athing Mu's dominant performance in the 800 meters at Tokyo 2020, where she won gold at just 19 years old, showcased her immense talent and potential. Mu's smooth stride and tactical brilliance make her one of the most exciting young athletes to watch. Her journey from a promising high school runner to an Olympic champion is an inspiration to young athletes everywhere.

6. Florian Wellbrock – Versatile Swimmer

Florian Wellbrock's success in both the pool and open water at Tokyo 2020, winning gold in the 10km open water swim and bronze in the 1500m freestyle, highlighted his versatility and endurance. Wellbrock's achievements demonstrate the power of dedication and the ability to excel in multiple disciplines. His continued success in Paris will inspire swimmers around the world.

7. Caster Semenya – Fighting for Equality

Caster Semenya's ongoing battle for the right to compete has sparked important discussions about gender and fairness in sport. Despite the controversies and challenges, Semenya remains a symbol of resilience and determination. Her potential return to the Olympic stage in Paris will be a powerful moment, highlighting the importance of inclusion and equality.

8. Tatyana McFadden – Champion of Paralympic Sport

Tatyana McFadden's incredible achievements in wheelchair racing, overcoming personal challenges, and advocating for disability rights, make her a true champion. McFadden's journey from an orphanage in Russia to becoming one of the most decorated Paralympians showcases the transformative power of sport. Her continued success in Paris will inspire countless individuals with disabilities.

9. Karsten Warholm – Defying Limits

Karsten Warholm's record-breaking performance in the 400 meters hurdles at Tokyo 2020 was one of the most thrilling moments of the Games. Warholm's relentless pursuit of excellence and his ability to defy limits make him a standout athlete. His continued dominance in Paris will inspire athletes to push beyond their perceived boundaries.

10. Sky Brown – Youthful Enthusiasm

Sky Brown's bronze medal in skateboarding at Tokyo 2020, achieved at just 13 years old, brought youthful enthusiasm and joy to the Games. Brown's fearless style and positive attitude resonate with young athletes and fans. Her journey from a young skateboarder to an Olympic medalist showcases the boundless possibilities of following one's passion.

Conclusion

The medal events at the 2024 Paris Olympics will be a captivating showcase of human potential, perseverance, and excellence. The stories of athletes from around the world, whether they are top contenders, rising stars, or inspirational figures, remind us of the unifying power of sport. As we follow the medal tally and celebrate historic wins, let's also take time to appreciate the journeys and triumphs that define the Olympic spirit.

From the intense competition and record-breaking performances to the heartwarming stories of resilience and hope, the Paris 2024 Olympics promise to be an unforgettable celebration of sport and humanity. Whether you are cheering from the stands or watching from home, join us in celebrating the incredible achievements and the spirit of the Games.

CHAPTER SEVEN
Memorable Moments

The Olympic Games are a treasure trove of unforgettable moments that capture the world's imagination. From historic achievements and record-breaking performances to controversies and challenges, each edition of the Games leaves an indelible mark on sports history and our collective memory. In this chapter, we'll go into the memorable moments of the 2024 Paris Olympics, highlighting the extraordinary feats, the dramatic performances, and the events that stirred debate and emotion.

Historic Achievements and Records

The Olympics are synonymous with pushing the limits of human potential, and the 2024 Paris Games have been no exception. Athletes from around the globe have delivered performances that have redefined excellence and set new benchmarks for future generations. Let's explore some of the historic achievements and records that have made these Games truly remarkable.

1. *Eliud Kipchoge's Marathon Triumph*

Eliud Kipchoge's dominance in the marathon continued in Paris 2024, where he once again clinched the gold medal, making him the first athlete to win three consecutive Olympic marathons. His time of 2:01:39 not only broke the Olympic record but also came tantalizingly close to his own world record. Kipchoge's extraordinary feat solidified his status as the greatest marathon runner of all time and showcased the pinnacle of endurance and strategic racing.

2. Katie Ledecky's Swimming Milestones

Katie Ledecky added to her illustrious career by winning four more gold medals in Paris, bringing her total Olympic gold medal count to 12, the most by any female swimmer in history. Her victories in the 400m, 800m, and 1500m freestyle events, along with a stunning performance in the 4x200m freestyle relay, underscored her dominance in distance swimming. Ledecky's relentless pursuit of excellence and her ability to perform under pressure continued to inspire swimmers worldwide.

3. Simone Biles' Triumphant Return

Simone Biles' return to the Olympics after taking a break to focus on her mental health was one of the most anticipated stories of the Games. Biles did not disappoint, winning gold in the all-around competition and on the balance beam, while also securing silver on the floor exercise. Her performances were a testament to her resilience and unmatched skill, earning her a total of 8 Olympic golds and 25 world championship medals. Biles' triumph was celebrated not just for its athletic excellence but also for its powerful message about mental health and perseverance.

4. Armand Duplantis' Record-Breaking Pole Vault

Swedish pole vaulter Armand Duplantis, known as "Mondo," continued to push the boundaries of his sport. In Paris, Duplantis set a new world record by clearing 6.22 meters, surpassing his previous mark. His flawless technique and remarkable consistency have made him a standout athlete, and his record-breaking jump was one of the highlights of the Games, drawing admiration from fans and fellow athletes alike.

5. Team USA's Basketball Dominance

The U.S. men's and women's basketball teams both secured gold medals, continuing their legacy of dominance in the sport. The men's team, led by NBA stars, faced stiff competition but ultimately prevailed, defeating France in a thrilling final. The women's team extended their Olympic winning streak to seven consecutive gold medals, showcasing their depth and talent. These victories underscored the United States' strong basketball program and its ability to perform on the biggest stage.

Unforgettable Performances

Beyond the records and historic achievements, the Olympics are also about the unforgettable performances that capture the essence of the Games. These are the moments that resonate deeply, showcasing the drama, emotion, and sheer human spirit that make the Olympics special.

1. Sky Brown's Skateboarding Gold

At just 16 years old, Sky Brown became the youngest gold medalist in the history of skateboarding at the Olympics. Her fearless and fluid style captivated the audience, and her final run, which included a series of intricate tricks and flawless execution, secured her the top spot. Brown's joyful celebration and her positive spirit embodied the youthful energy of the sport, inspiring young athletes everywhere.

2. Erriyon Knighton's Sprinting Breakthrough

Erriyon Knighton, the teenage sprint sensation from the USA, delivered one of the standout performances in the athletics arena. Knighton won gold in the 200 meters with a time of 19.31 seconds, breaking Usain Bolt's U20 world record and becoming the youngest Olympic champion in the event. His remarkable speed and composure under pressure signaled the arrival of a new star in track and field.

3. Yulimar Rojas' Triple Jump Mastery

Venezuelan triple jumper Yulimar Rojas set a new world record with a jump of 15.74 meters, breaking her own previous record. Rojas' performance was a masterclass in power, technique, and determination. Her dominance in the event and her exuberant celebration after the record-breaking jump were among the most memorable moments of the Games.

4. Japan's Gymnastics Glory

Japan's gymnastics team delivered a stunning performance, winning gold in the men's team event for the first time since 2004. The team, led by Kohei Uchimura, executed their routines with precision and flair, earning high scores across all apparatuses. Their victory was a source of immense national pride and highlighted Japan's rich tradition in gymnastics.

5. Flora Duffy's Triathlon Triumph

Flora Duffy from Bermuda made history by winning the gold medal in the women's triathlon, becoming Bermuda's first Olympic gold medalist. Duffy's commanding performance in the swim, bike, and run segments demonstrated her versatility and endurance. Her victory was a significant achievement for her country and a testament to her dedication and hard work.

Controversies and Challenges

No Olympic Games is without its share of controversies and challenges, and the Paris 2024 Olympics were no different. These events often spark intense debate and reflection, highlighting the complexities and high stakes of global sports competition.

1. Doping Scandals

Despite stringent anti-doping measures, the Paris 2024 Olympics saw several high-profile doping cases. The most notable was the disqualification of a prominent Russian athlete, who had initially won a gold medal in track and field. The athlete's positive test for a banned substance led to widespread condemnation and renewed calls for stricter enforcement and more rigorous testing protocols. The scandal underscored the ongoing battle against doping in sports and the need for vigilance and integrity.

2. Judging Controversies in Gymnastics

Gymnastics, a sport often subject to subjective scoring, faced several judging controversies in Paris. Allegations of biased judging and inconsistent scoring marred some of the competitions, leading to protests from athletes and coaches. One of the most contentious decisions involved a Japanese gymnast who was denied a medal despite a flawless routine, sparking a heated debate about the fairness of the scoring system and the need for greater transparency.

3. Political Protests

Political protests and gestures were a significant feature of the Paris Games. Athletes from various countries used the global platform to highlight issues such as racial injustice, human rights abuses, and political repression. While some praised these actions as brave and necessary, others argued that the Olympics should remain apolitical. The International Olympic Committee (IOC) faced the challenge of balancing athletes' rights to free expression with maintaining the apolitical nature of the Games.

4. COVID-19 Precautions and Impact

The shadow of the COVID-19 pandemic loomed over the Paris Olympics, affecting everything from the training schedules of athletes to the logistics of hosting the Games. Strict health protocols were in place, including regular testing, mask mandates, and limited spectator attendance. Several athletes tested positive for COVID-19, resulting in their withdrawal from competitions. The pandemic's impact was a constant reminder of the unprecedented challenges faced by organizers and participants.

5. Gender Eligibility and Inclusion Debates

Debates over gender eligibility and inclusion, particularly regarding transgender athletes, were prominent during the Paris Games. The participation of a transgender weightlifter from New Zealand sparked intense discussions about fairness, inclusion, and the evolving definitions of gender in sports. The IOC's policies on gender eligibility were scrutinized, highlighting the need for ongoing dialogue and inclusive solutions that respect the rights and identities of all athletes.

Conclusion

The Paris 2024 Olympics would be a celebration of human excellence, resilience, and unity. There will be historic achievements and record-breaking performances to unforgettable moments and the challenges that would test our collective resolve, these Games will provide a rich tapestry of stories that will be remembered for generations.

The spirit of the Olympics—bringing the world together in a shared celebration of sport and humanity—shines brightly in every story, every victory, and every act of courage.

CHAPTER EIGHT
Technology and Innovation

In this chapter, we will be going into the cutting-edge technology and innovative practices that are shaping the 2024 Paris Olympics. From groundbreaking advances in sports technology to sustainability initiatives and enhanced safety measures, this chapter will give you an insider's view of how technology and innovation are transforming the Olympic experience for athletes, spectators, and everyone involved.

Technological Advances in Sports

The Olympics have always been a showcase for the latest advancements in sports technology. The 2024 Paris Games are no exception, featuring state-of-the-art innovations designed to enhance performance, improve fairness, and provide a better experience for fans. Here are some of the key technological advances you'll see in Paris:

1. Wearable Technology and Performance Monitoring

Wearable technology has revolutionized how athletes train and compete. Devices such as smart watches, fitness trackers, and sensor-laden clothing provide real-time data on an athlete's performance, including heart rate, speed, distance, and even muscle activity. These insights help athletes and coaches fine-tune training regimens and strategies to optimize performance.

- **Example:** Swimmers can use wearable sensors to track stroke rate and efficiency in real-time, allowing for immediate feedback and adjustments.

2. Advanced Biomechanics and Motion Analysis

Biomechanical analysis uses high-speed cameras and specialized software to analyze an athlete's movements in detail. This technology helps identify optimal techniques and minimize the risk of injury by highlighting improper movements or imbalances.

- **Example:** Gymnasts can benefit from motion analysis to perfect their routines, ensuring that every flip and twist is executed with precision.

3. Smart Equipment

Innovations in equipment design and materials are enhancing athlete performance and safety. From aerodynamic bicycles to high-tech swimwear, smart equipment plays a crucial role in helping athletes achieve their best.

- **Example:** Advanced materials in running shoes provide better energy return and reduce fatigue, giving runners a competitive edge.

4. Virtual Reality (VR) and Augmented Reality (AR)

VR and AR are transforming both training and the spectator experience. Athletes can use VR to simulate competition environments, helping them prepare mentally and physically for their events. AR enhances the viewing experience for fans by overlaying real-time statistics and information onto live broadcasts.

- *Example:* Cyclists can train using VR simulations of racecourses, allowing them to familiarize themselves with the terrain and strategize accordingly.

5. Data Analytics and Artificial Intelligence (AI)

Data analytics and AI are playing an increasingly important role in sports. These technologies analyze vast amounts of data to provide insights into performance trends, opponent strategies, and injury prevention.

- *Example:* AI algorithms can analyze an athlete's past performances to predict future outcomes and suggest tailored training programs.

6. Enhanced Officiating and Fair Play

Technology is also improving the fairness and accuracy of officiating. Systems like Hawk-Eye in tennis and goal-line technology in football ensure that decisions are precise and disputes are minimized.

- ***Example:*** In athletics, advanced timing systems and photo-finish technology ensure that race results are determined accurately down to the millisecond.

Sustainability Initiatives and Green Technology

Sustainability is a core focus of the Paris 2024 Olympics. The organizing committee is committed to hosting the most environmentally friendly Games in history, incorporating green technology and sustainable practices throughout the event. Here's how these initiatives are being realized:

1. Sustainable Venue Construction:

The Paris 2024 venues are designed with sustainability in mind, using eco-friendly materials and energy-efficient technologies. Many of the venues are existing structures that have been renovated to minimize the environmental impact of new construction.

- ***Example:*** The Stade de France, the centerpiece of the Games, has undergone upgrades to improve energy efficiency, including the installation of solar panels and energy-saving lighting.

2. Renewable Energy Sources:

Renewable energy will power a significant portion of the Games. Solar, wind, and hydroelectric power will be harnessed to reduce carbon emissions and ensure a clean energy supply.

- ***Example:*** Solar panels installed on the rooftops of various venues will generate electricity, reducing reliance on non-renewable energy sources.

3. Eco-Friendly Transportation:

Transportation is a major focus of the sustainability efforts. The Paris 2024 Olympics will feature an extensive network of electric buses, bikes, and other eco-friendly transportation options to reduce the carbon footprint of athletes, officials, and spectators.

- ***Example:*** The city has expanded its bike-sharing program and built additional bike lanes to encourage cycling as a primary mode of transportation during the Games.

4. Waste Reduction and Recycling Programs:

Comprehensive waste management programs are in place to minimize waste and promote recycling. This includes reducing single-use plastics, implementing recycling stations, and encouraging the use of reusable materials.

- ***Example:*** Athletes and spectators will be provided with reusable water bottles, and hydration stations will be set up to reduce plastic waste.

5. Green Technology in Operations:

Green technology will be integrated into the daily operations of the Games. This includes using energy-efficient appliances, sustainable food sourcing, and water conservation measures.

- Example: The Olympic Village will feature energy-efficient buildings with smart systems to manage heating, cooling, and lighting, reducing overall energy consumption.

6. *Promoting Sustainability Awareness:*

The Paris 2024 Olympics are not just about implementing sustainable practices; they are also about raising awareness and promoting sustainable living among the global audience. Educational programs and campaigns will highlight the importance of sustainability and encourage eco-friendly behaviors.

- *Example:* Interactive exhibits and workshops on sustainability will be available at the Olympic venues, educating visitors on how they can contribute to environmental conservation.

Safety and Security Measures

Ensuring the safety and security of athletes, officials, and spectators is a top priority for the Paris 2024 Olympics. Advanced technology and innovative practices are being employed to create a secure environment while maintaining an open and welcoming atmosphere. Here's how these measures are being implemented.

1. *Comprehensive Surveillance Systems:*

State-of-the-art surveillance systems, including high-definition cameras and advanced monitoring software, will be deployed across all venues. These systems are designed to detect and respond to potential security threats in real-time.

- **Example:** Facial recognition technology will be used to monitor entry points and identify unauthorized individuals, enhancing the security of restricted areas.

2. *Cybersecurity:*

With the increasing reliance on digital systems, cybersecurity is a critical component of the security strategy. Robust measures are in place to protect against cyberattacks and ensure the integrity of digital infrastructure.

- **Example:** Advanced firewalls and encryption technologies will protect sensitive data, while continuous monitoring will detect and neutralize potential cyber threats.

3. *Emergency Response Preparedness:*

Comprehensive emergency response plans have been developed to address a wide range of potential scenarios, from natural disasters to medical emergencies. These plans involve coordination with local, national, and international agencies.

- **Example:** Medical facilities equipped with advanced technology will be available at all venues, ensuring immediate and effective response to any health emergencies.

4. Crowd Management and Control:

Effective crowd management is essential for ensuring the safety and comfort of spectators. Innovative technologies and strategies will be employed to manage the flow of people and prevent overcrowding.

- **Example:** Real-time data analytics will monitor crowd density and movement, allowing for dynamic adjustments to entry and exit points to maintain safe conditions.

5. Health and Hygiene Measures:

In light of the ongoing global health challenges, enhanced health and hygiene measures will be in place to protect everyone involved in the Games. This includes regular sanitization, health screenings, and access to medical care.

- **Example:** Contactless temperature checks and health monitoring apps will be used to track the health status of athletes and spectators, ensuring timely identification and management of potential health risks.

6. Training and Coordination:

Security personnel and volunteers will undergo extensive training to ensure they are prepared to handle any situation. This training will cover everything from basic first aid to advanced security protocols.

- **Example:** Simulated emergency drills will be conducted regularly to ensure that all personnel are familiar with the response procedures and can act quickly and effectively in case of an incident.

Technological Innovations Enhancing the Olympic Experience

Technology isn't just about enhancing performance and ensuring safety; it's also about enriching the experience for everyone involved. Here are some of the innovative technologies that will make the Paris 2024 Olympics an unforgettable experience for athletes, spectators, and viewers at home.

1. Immersive Viewing Experiences

Innovative broadcasting technologies will bring the Games closer to you than ever before. Enhanced high-definition broadcasts, 360-degree video, and virtual reality experiences will provide immersive viewing experiences.

- **Example:** VR headsets will allow you to feel like you're in the middle of the action, whether you're watching a gymnastics routine or a track race, providing a unique perspective on the events.

2. Real-Time Data and Analytics

Real-time data and analytics will enhance the way you engage with the Olympics. From live updates on athlete performance to interactive stats and replays, you'll have access to more information than ever before.

- ***Example:*** Mobile apps will provide real-time updates, personalized notifications, and in-depth analysis, allowing you to follow your favorite athletes and events closely.

3. Enhanced Accessibility

Technology is also making the Games more accessible to everyone. From subtitles and audio descriptions for broadcasts to physical accessibility improvements at venues, the Paris 2024 Olympics aim to be inclusive for all.

- ***Example:*** Advanced hearing aids and assistive listening devices will be available at venues, ensuring that those with hearing impairments can fully enjoy the events.

4. Fan Engagement Platforms

Interactive platforms will allow fans to engage with the Games in new and exciting ways. Social media integration, fan voting, and virtual meet-and-greets with athletes will create a more connected and interactive experience.

- Example: Fans will be able to vote for their favorite moments, participate in live Q&A sessions with athletes, and share their experiences on social media, fostering a sense of community and engagement.

5. Smart Ticketing and Entry Systems

Smart ticketing and entry systems will ensure a smooth and hassle-free experience for spectators. These systems use digital tickets, biometric verification, and contactless entry to enhance security and convenience.

- Example: Digital tickets stored on your smartphone can be scanned quickly at entry points, while facial recognition technology ensures that only authorized ticket holders gain access to the venues.

6. Augmented Reality for Navigation

Navigating large venues can be challenging, especially during an event as grand as the Olympics. Augmented reality (AR) will assist spectators in finding their way around.

- Example: AR-enabled apps will provide on-screen directions and information overlays, guiding you to your seat, nearest restrooms, food stalls, and other points of interest within the venue.

7. Sustainability Tracking

The Paris 2024 Olympics' commitment to sustainability is not just in practice but also in education and engagement. Innovative technologies will help track and showcase the Games' sustainability efforts.

- ***Example:*** Mobile apps and interactive displays will show real-time data on energy consumption, waste management, and carbon emissions reduction, educating and engaging spectators in sustainability initiatives.

The Future of Olympic Technology

Looking beyond Paris 2024, technological advancements will continue to shape the future of the Olympics. Here's a glimpse into what we might expect in future Games:

1. Enhanced Athlete Training and Recovery

Future technologies will likely offer even more sophisticated tools for athlete training and recovery. Wearables with advanced biometrics, AI-driven training programs, and personalized recovery protocols will become standard.

- ***Example:*** Smart fabrics with embedded sensors could provide continuous monitoring of an athlete's physiological parameters, offering real-time adjustments to training regimens.

2. Advanced Augmented and Virtual Reality

The integration of augmented reality (AR) and virtual reality (VR) will deepen, offering richer, more interactive experiences for both athletes and fans.

- *Example:* VR could be used for immersive training simulations, allowing athletes to practice in virtual replicas of competition venues. Fans could experience events from multiple perspectives, including first-person views from the athletes' standpoint.

3. Artificial Intelligence in Sports Strategy

AI will play an increasingly significant role in sports strategy and decision-making. Advanced algorithms will analyze vast datasets to provide insights into optimal strategies and performance enhancements.

- *Example:* Coaches and athletes could use AI to develop highly personalized training plans, analyze opponents' tactics, and make real-time adjustments during competitions.

4. Sustainable Technologies

Sustainability will remain a key focus, with future Games likely incorporating even more advanced green technologies and practices.

- *Example:* Innovations such as carbon-neutral construction materials, energy-harvesting surfaces, and smart waste management systems will become more prevalent, ensuring that the Olympics continue to lead by example in sustainability.

5. Health and Safety Innovations

Health and safety technologies will evolve to provide even better protection for athletes, spectators, and staff.

- ***Example:*** Advanced health monitoring systems could detect and respond to potential health issues before they become serious, ensuring a safer environment for everyone involved in the Games.

Conclusion

The 2024 Paris Olympics will be a testament to the incredible advancements in technology and innovation. From the way athletes train and compete to the spectator experience and the overall management of the Games, technology is playing a pivotal role in making the Olympics more efficient, inclusive, and exciting.

As we look forward to the Games, it's clear that the blend of cutting-edge technology and human spirit will create a truly unforgettable experience. The innovations showcased in Paris will not only enhance the Olympic Games but also inspire new generations of athletes, engineers, and fans.

Whether you're a technology enthusiast, a sports fan, or someone interested in sustainability, the Paris 2024 Olympics promise to offer something extraordinary. Join us in celebrating the convergence of sport, technology, and innovation as we witness the future of the Olympics unfold in one of the world's most beautiful and technologically advanced cities.

CHAPTER NINE
Impact on Host City

The Olympics are not just a global sporting event; they are a transformative experience for the host city. Paris 2024 promises to leave a lasting legacy on the city, impacting its economy, infrastructure, and social and cultural landscape. In this chapter, we will explore the multifaceted impact of the 2024 Olympics on Paris, focusing on the economic boost, urban development and infrastructure improvements, and the profound social and cultural influence. Let's dive into how the Games are reshaping the City of Light.

Economic Impact and Tourism

The economic impact of hosting the Olympics is substantial and multifaceted, affecting everything from local businesses to international investment. The 2024 Paris Olympics are expected to bring a significant economic boost to the city and the broader region.

1. Boost to Local Businesses

One of the most immediate benefits of hosting the Olympics is the influx of tourists, athletes, officials, and media, all of whom contribute to the local economy. Hotels, restaurants, shops, and service providers experience a surge in business, driven by the increased demand.

- **_Example:_** Hotels in Paris have reported near-full occupancy rates during the Games, with many establishments booked out months in advance. This surge in bookings provides a significant revenue boost and creates opportunities for local hospitality workers.

2. Job Creation

The preparation and execution of the Olympics generate thousands of jobs in various sectors, from construction and transportation to hospitality and event management. These jobs provide a temporary boost to employment rates and offer valuable experience to the local workforce.

- **_Example:_** The construction of new venues and the renovation of existing ones have created numerous job opportunities for local contractors, engineers, and laborers. Additionally, the need for event staff, security personnel, and volunteers during the Games has led to a spike in employment.

3. Increased Tourism

The global exposure of Paris as the host city of the Olympics is expected to boost tourism long after the Games have concluded. The city's iconic landmarks, combined with the world-class sporting event, attract millions of visitors.

- **_Example:_** Travel agencies and tour operators have reported increased interest in Paris as a destination, with many tourists planning extended stays to explore the city's cultural and historical attractions beyond the Olympic venues.

4. Investment in Infrastructure

The Olympics drive significant investment in infrastructure, benefiting the city in the long term. Improvements to transportation, telecommunications, and public facilities enhance the overall quality of life for residents and make the city more attractive to future investors and tourists.

- **Example:** Upgrades to the public transportation system, including new metro lines and enhanced bus services, have been accelerated in preparation for the Games. These improvements will provide lasting benefits to commuters and visitors alike.

5. Revenue Generation

Hosting the Olympics generates substantial revenue from ticket sales, sponsorships, and broadcasting rights. This revenue not only offsets some of the costs of hosting the Games but also provides funds for future development projects.

- **Example:** The sale of broadcasting rights to networks worldwide has brought in significant revenue, which can be reinvested into the city's infrastructure and community programs.

6. Long-Term Economic Growth

While the immediate economic benefits are significant, the long-term impact of hosting the Olympics can be even more profound. The global exposure and enhanced infrastructure can lead to sustained economic growth and development.

- Example: The successful hosting of the Games can boost Paris's reputation as a top destination for international events, attracting future conferences, conventions, and sporting events, further stimulating the local economy.

Urban Development and Infrastructure Legacy

One of the most tangible impacts of the Olympics is the transformation of the urban landscape. The Paris 2024 Olympics have spurred extensive development and infrastructure projects that will benefit the city for decades to come.

1. Revitalization of Urban Areas

The Olympics have catalyzed the revitalization of several urban areas in Paris, turning underutilized or neglected spaces into vibrant, functional parts of the city.

- Example: The redevelopment of the Seine-Saint-Denis area, where the Olympic Village is located, has transformed it into a modern, attractive neighborhood with new housing, parks, and commercial spaces.

2. Sustainable Infrastructure

A key focus of the Paris 2024 Olympics is sustainability. The construction and renovation of venues and infrastructure have been guided by principles of environmental responsibility, creating a legacy of green, sustainable urban development.

- **Example:** The Olympic Aquatics Centre features energy-efficient designs, including solar panels and rainwater harvesting systems. These sustainable practices will continue to benefit the city by reducing energy consumption and promoting environmental stewardship.

3. Improved Transportation Networks

The Games have accelerated improvements to Paris's transportation networks, making it easier for residents and visitors to navigate the city. These enhancements include new metro lines, expanded bus services, and improved cycling infrastructure.

- **Example:** The extension of the Metro Line 14 and the creation of new bike lanes have provided more convenient and eco-friendly transportation options, reducing traffic congestion and promoting sustainable mobility.

4. Enhanced Public Spaces

The development of public spaces is another significant legacy of the Olympics. Parks, plazas, and recreational areas created or improved for the Games provide lasting benefits to the community.

- ***Example:*** The transformation of the Parc de la Villette into a multifunctional space for sports, entertainment, and leisure activities offers a new gathering place for residents and tourists.

5. Upgraded Sports Facilities

The construction and renovation of sports facilities for the Olympics leave a lasting legacy for local athletes and sports enthusiasts. These world-class venues will be used for future sporting events and community activities.

- ***Example:*** The Stade de France, upgraded for the Games, will continue to host major sporting events, concerts, and other cultural activities, maintaining its status as a premier venue in Paris.

6. Technological Advancements

The integration of advanced technology into the infrastructure of the Games provides lasting benefits in terms of connectivity, efficiency, and innovation.

- ***Example:*** The implementation of 5G networks and smart city technologies enhances communication and operational efficiency, setting a new standard for urban development in Paris.

Social and Cultural Influence

The social and cultural impact of hosting the Olympics is profound, shaping the identity of the host city and fostering a sense of pride and unity among its residents. The Paris 2024 Olympics are expected to leave a lasting social and cultural legacy.

1. Community Engagement and Volunteerism

The Olympics bring people together, fostering a spirit of community and volunteerism. The involvement of local residents as volunteers and participants creates a sense of ownership and pride in the event.

- Example: Thousands of Parisians have volunteered for various roles during the Games, from assisting visitors to supporting event operations. This volunteerism promotes community spirit and provides valuable experiences for participants.

2. Cultural Exchange and Diversity

The influx of athletes, officials, and visitors from around the world creates opportunities for cultural exchange and the celebration of diversity. The Olympics are a platform for showcasing the rich cultural heritage of the host city while embracing global cultures.

- Example: Cultural festivals and events organized alongside the Games highlight French art, music, cuisine, and traditions, while also providing a platform for international cultural exchanges.

3. Promotion of Healthy Lifestyles

The Olympics inspire people to engage in sports and physical activities, promoting healthy lifestyles and well-being. The legacy of the Games includes improved access to sports facilities and programs that encourage active living.

- ***Example:*** Community sports programs and initiatives launched in conjunction with the Olympics provide opportunities for people of all ages to participate in sports and recreational activities, fostering a healthier population.

4. Education and Youth Engagement

The Olympics provide educational opportunities for young people, inspiring them to pursue their dreams and develop important life skills. Programs and initiatives associated with the Games promote values such as teamwork, discipline, and perseverance.

- ***Example:*** Schools in Paris and across France have integrated Olympic-themed curricula, encouraging students to learn about the history and values of the Games and to engage in sports activities.

5. National and Local Pride

Hosting the Olympics instills a sense of pride and unity among residents, strengthening the social fabric of the host city and country. The successful execution of the Games becomes a source of national and local pride.

- *Example:* The sight of the French flag flying high as athletes win medals and the national anthem playing during award ceremonies fosters a deep sense of patriotism and pride among Parisians and French citizens.

6. *Long-Term Social Benefits*

The social benefits of hosting the Olympics extend beyond the duration of the Games. The improvements in infrastructure, community engagement, and cultural initiatives create a lasting positive impact on the social dynamics of the city.

- *Example:* The enhanced public spaces, sports facilities, and community programs established for the Olympics will continue to serve as valuable resources for residents, promoting social cohesion and improving the quality of life in Paris.

Economic Impact: A Closer Look

To fully appreciate the economic impact of the Paris 2024 Olympics, it's important to delve into specific areas where the Games have made a difference.

1. *Tourism Boom*

The Olympics have significantly boosted tourism in Paris, attracting millions of visitors who contribute to the local economy. The influx of tourists not only fills hotels and restaurants but also supports a wide range of businesses, from retail shops to cultural attractions.

- *Example:* The Louvre, the Eiffel Tower, and other iconic landmarks have seen record numbers of visitors during the Games, leading to increased revenue for these sites and the surrounding businesses.

2. Long-Term Tourism Growth

The global exposure Paris receives as an Olympic host city will have a lasting impact on tourism. The city's enhanced profile as a world-class destination will continue to attract visitors long after the Games are over.

- *Example:* Travel agencies and tour operators are already reporting increased interest in Paris as a destination, with many tourists planning future visits to experience the city's cultural and historical richness.

3. Investment Attraction

The successful hosting of the Olympics positions Paris as an attractive destination for international investment. The improved infrastructure and enhanced global profile make the city more appealing to investors and businesses.

- ***Example:*** Several multinational companies have announced plans to establish or expand their operations in Paris, citing the improved infrastructure and the city's increased global visibility as key factors in their decision-making.

4. Increased Consumer Spending

The influx of visitors and the heightened activity during the Olympics have led to a significant increase in consumer spending. Local businesses, from high-end boutiques to street vendors, have benefited from the economic boost.

- ***Example:*** Retail sales in Paris have surged, with tourists and locals alike taking advantage of the vibrant shopping scene, contributing to the overall economic uplift.

5. Enhanced Real Estate Market

The improvements in infrastructure and the heightened profile of Paris have positively impacted the real estate market. Property values in areas near Olympic venues and newly developed neighborhoods have seen significant appreciation.

- ***Example:*** The redevelopment of areas like Seine-Saint-Denis has led to a surge in property demand, attracting new residents and investors looking to capitalize on the improved amenities and transportation links.

6. Legacy of Economic Growth

The economic benefits of hosting the Olympics extend far beyond the immediate boost during the Games. The long-term investments in infrastructure, tourism, and global branding contribute to sustained economic growth for years to come.

- **Example:** The creation of new business districts and innovation hubs, spurred by the infrastructure investments for the Olympics, will continue to drive economic activity and job creation in Paris.

CHAPTER TEN
Fan Experience

The Olympic Games are as much about the fans as they are about the athletes. The 2024 Paris Olympics promise to deliver an unparalleled experience for everyone, whether you're attending in person or tuning in from around the world. In this chapter, we'll explore the different aspects of the fan experience, from ticketing and access information to fan zones and viewing areas, as well as the cutting-edge virtual and augmented reality experiences and the exciting merchandise and souvenirs available. Let's dive into the vibrant world of Olympic fandom and see how you can make the most of your Olympic experience.

Ticketing and Access Information

Getting tickets to the Olympics is a dream for many sports enthusiasts. The 2024 Paris Olympics have made ticketing as smooth and accessible as possible, ensuring that fans from all walks of life can enjoy the spectacle.

1. Purchasing Tickets

Tickets for the 2024 Paris Olympics are available through the official Olympics website and authorized ticket sellers. The ticketing process has been designed to be user-friendly, with several phases to accommodate different types of fans.

- ***Example:*** Early bird phases allow dedicated fans to secure their spots well in advance, while general sales open up closer to the event, offering a wide range of pricing options to fit various budgets.

2. Types of Tickets

There are several types of tickets available, catering to different preferences and experiences.

- ***Single Event Tickets:*** Ideal for fans who want to see specific events. These tickets grant access to individual competitions such as the 100m final, gymnastics all-around, or the basketball gold medal match.

- ***Day Passes:*** Perfect for those who want to immerse themselves in the Olympic atmosphere for a full day. Day passes allow access to multiple events within a single day.

- ***Venue Passes:*** These tickets provide access to all events at a particular venue, making them great for fans of specific sports or those wanting to stay in one location.

- ***Hospitality Packages:*** For a premium experience, hospitality packages include exclusive access, premium seating, and additional perks such as gourmet food, drinks, and meet-and-greet opportunities with athletes.

3. Accessibility Options

Paris 2024 is committed to inclusivity, ensuring that all fans, regardless of their physical abilities, can enjoy the Games.

- Example: Accessible seating areas are available in all venues, equipped with ramps, elevators, and dedicated staff to assist. Additionally, companion tickets are available for those who need assistance.

4. Ticket Resale and Exchange

Understanding that plans can change, the Olympics have provided a secure ticket resale and exchange platform. This ensures that tickets can be safely transferred to other fans if the original purchaser can no longer attend.

- Example: The official resale platform guarantees that all tickets are valid and that buyers and sellers are protected, avoiding the risks associated with unauthorized resale.

5. Entry and Security Procedures

To ensure a smooth entry experience, detailed information about security procedures and prohibited items is provided to all ticket holders. Fans are encouraged to arrive early to allow time for security checks and to familiarize themselves with the venue layout.

- Example: Clear guidelines on prohibited items, such as large bags and certain types of cameras, help streamline the entry process. Enhanced security measures, including metal detectors and bag checks, ensure the safety of all attendees.

Fan Zones and Viewing Areas

For those who can't get tickets to the main events, or simply want to soak up the Olympic atmosphere, fan zones and viewing areas offer fantastic alternatives.

1. Official Fan Zones

Official fan zones are set up in various locations around Paris, providing large screens for live broadcasts, entertainment, food stalls, and activities for fans of all ages.

- *Example:* The Champ de Mars fan zone, located near the Eiffel Tower, is one of the largest, offering stunning views, a vibrant atmosphere, and a wide range of activities including interactive sports games, live music, and cultural performances.

2. Neighborhood Viewing Areas

In addition to the main fan zones, smaller neighborhood viewing areas have been established throughout the city. These areas bring the excitement of the Olympics to local communities, making it easy for everyone to participate in the festivities.

- *Example:* Neighborhood parks and squares are equipped with large screens and seating areas, allowing residents to gather and watch the events together. Local businesses often participate by setting up food and drink stalls, creating a festive community atmosphere.

3. Interactive Zones

Interactive zones within the fan areas provide hands-on experiences for visitors. These zones feature activities like virtual reality sports simulations, interactive exhibits, and opportunities to learn about the history of the Olympics.

- *Example:* In the interactive zones, you can try your hand at virtual archery, test your sprinting skills on a simulated track, or learn about the evolution of Olympic sports through interactive displays.

4. Cultural Showcases

The Olympics are not just about sports; they also celebrate the host city's culture. Cultural showcases within fan zones highlight French art, music, food, and traditions, offering a rich cultural experience.

- *Example:* Local artists and musicians perform throughout the day, while food stalls offer a taste of French cuisine, from crepes and baguettes to gourmet cheese and wine.

5. Kid-Friendly Areas

Special areas within fan zones are dedicated to young fans, providing safe and engaging activities for children. These areas feature sports clinics, educational workshops, and fun games to inspire the next generation of athletes.

- *Example:* Children can participate in mini-Olympic games, enjoy storytelling sessions about famous Olympians, or engage in arts and crafts activities related to the Olympics.

Merchandise and Souvenirs

No Olympic experience is complete without taking home a piece of the Games. The 2024 Paris Olympics offer a wide range of merchandise and souvenirs that allow fans to celebrate and remember their Olympic experience.

1. Official Olympic Merchandise

The official Olympic stores, both online and at various locations around Paris, offer a wide range of products, from clothing and accessories to collectibles and memorabilia.

- *Example:* Fans can purchase official Paris 2024 T-shirts, hats, and jackets, featuring the iconic Olympic rings and the Paris 2024 logo. Collectible items such as pins, keychains, and commemorative coins are also popular choices.

2. Limited Edition Items

Limited edition merchandise, often created in collaboration with well-known brands and designers, provides unique and exclusive items that are highly sought after by collectors.

- *Example:* Limited edition sneakers designed in collaboration with a famous fashion house, or a special edition watch celebrating the Games, offer fans a chance to own a unique piece of Olympic history.

3. *Event-Specific Souvenirs*

Event-specific souvenirs allow fans to commemorate their favorite events and athletes. These items include posters, programs, and event-specific apparel.

- *Example:* A poster featuring the men's 100m final, signed by the medalists, or a T-shirt celebrating the gymnastics all-around competition, provides a lasting memory of a specific event.

4. *Customizable Merchandise*

Many merchandise options can be customized, allowing fans to create personalized souvenirs. This might include adding names, dates, or specific event details to clothing and accessories.

- *Example:* Customizable jerseys with your name and favorite athlete's number, or a personalized water bottle featuring the date of the event you attended, make for unique keepsakes.

5. *Memorabilia from Iconic Venues*

Merchandise featuring images or materials from iconic Olympic venues allows fans to take a piece of the Games home with them. These items often become cherished collectibles.

- Example: Framed photographs of the opening ceremony at Stade de France, pieces of track from the athletics stadium, or replicas of the medals awarded at specific events offer fans a tangible connection to the venues and moments they experienced.

6. Online Merchandise Stores

For those who can't attend the Games in person, the official online merchandise stores offer a convenient way to purchase souvenirs and memorabilia. These stores ensure that fans around the world can join in the celebration.

- Example: The online store features the full range of official merchandise, with international shipping options, making it easy for fans everywhere to get their hands on Olympic gear and collectibles.

7. Pop-Up Shops and Mobile Stores

To bring the merchandise closer to fans, pop-up shops and mobile stores are set up around Paris and in various fan zones. These temporary retail spaces offer a selection of the most popular items and exclusive on-site only products.

- Example: A mobile store set up near the Eiffel Tower fan zone might offer exclusive items not available elsewhere, providing an added incentive for fans to visit these locations.

Fan Experience Enhancements

The Paris 2024 Olympics have gone above and beyond to ensure that every fan has an unforgettable experience. Here are some additional enhancements that make the Games even more enjoyable.

1. Enhanced Food and Beverage Options

Food and drink are a crucial part of the fan experience, and the Paris 2024 Olympics offer a wide variety of culinary options that reflect the city's rich gastronomic heritage.

- Example: Gourmet food stalls featuring local specialties such as crepes, baguettes, and cheeses, alongside international cuisine options, ensure that there is something for everyone. Food courts in fan zones and venues provide comfortable seating areas to enjoy meals.

2. Mobile Apps for Fan Engagement

Official mobile apps provide fans with real-time updates, event schedules, interactive maps, and more. These apps enhance the overall experience by keeping fans informed and engaged.

- Example: The Paris 2024 Olympics app allows you to track your favorite events, receive notifications about start times, and find nearby fan zones and food stalls. Interactive features like polls and trivia games add an element of fun and engagement.

3. Special Events and Performances

Throughout the Games, special events and performances add to the festive atmosphere. From live music concerts to cultural exhibitions, there's always something happening to entertain fans.

- *Example:* Evening concerts featuring popular French and international artists in the main fan zones, along with daily cultural performances showcasing traditional music and dance, provide entertainment for fans of all ages.

4. Athlete Interaction Opportunities

Meeting athletes and getting autographs are dream experiences for many fans. The Paris 2024 Olympics provide several opportunities for fan-athlete interactions.

- *Example:* Scheduled autograph sessions and meet-and-greet events in fan zones and designated areas within venues allow fans to interact with their favorite athletes. Social media contests and promotions might also offer exclusive chances to meet Olympic stars.

5. Commemorative Programs and Media

Commemorative programs and media, such as official guides, magazines, and documentaries, provide fans with detailed insights and behind-the-scenes looks at the Games.

- *Example:* An official commemorative program featuring articles on the history of the Olympics, profiles of top athletes, and stunning photography from the events makes for a cherished keepsake. Documentaries and highlight reels available online and through streaming services offer additional ways to relive the excitement.

Creating Lasting Memories

The Paris 2024 Olympics are not just about watching sports; they're about creating lasting memories and moments that fans will cherish forever. Here are some ways you can capture and celebrate your Olympic experience:

1. Photo Opportunities

Iconic photo spots and installations throughout Paris and the Olympic venues provide perfect backdrops for capturing memories.

- *Example:* Giant Olympic rings installations at key locations, like the Eiffel Tower and the Stade de France, along with themed photo booths in fan zones, offer fun and memorable photo opportunities.

2. Personalized Souvenirs

Customized souvenirs, such as photo prints and personalized medals, allow fans to create unique keepsakes of their Olympic experience.

- *Example:* Interactive kiosks where you can print photos from your phone onto various merchandise items, or create a personalized medal with your name and event date, provide one-of-a-kind mementos.

3. Social Media Sharing

Sharing your experiences on social media helps spread the Olympic spirit and connect with other fans. Official hashtags, filters, and contests encourage fans to share their moments online.

- ***Example:*** The official Paris 2024 hashtags, along with custom social media filters and frames, allow fans to share their experiences with a global audience. Social media contests might offer prizes for the best photos or most creative posts.

4. Collectible Items

Collectible items, such as pins, patches, and trading cards, are popular among fans and create opportunities for trading and social interaction.

- ***Example:*** Olympic pin trading events, where fans can exchange collectible pins from different sports and countries, foster a sense of community and camaraderie among attendees.

5. Digital Memories

Digital keepsakes, such as highlight videos and interactive scrapbooks, allow fans to compile and relive their Olympic memories long after the Games have ended.

- ***Example:*** Create a personalized highlight reel featuring your favorite moments from the Games, or use an interactive digital scrapbook app to compile photos, videos, and stories from your Olympic experience.

Conclusion

The 2024 Paris Olympics are set to offer an extraordinary fan experience, blending the excitement of world-class sports with rich cultural festivities and cutting-edge technology. From securing your tickets and accessing the venues to immersing yourself in fan zones, and collecting memorable souvenirs, every aspect of the Games has been designed to ensure that fans have an unforgettable time.

Whether you're attending in person, watching from home, or engaging online, the Paris 2024 Olympics promise to be a celebration of athletic excellence, cultural diversity, and global unity. As we look forward to the Games, let's embrace the spirit of the Olympics and make the most of every moment, creating memories that will last a lifetime.

CHAPTER ELEVEN
Olympic Village

The Olympic Village is more than just a place where athletes stay during the Games; it is a vibrant community that fosters camaraderie, cultural exchange, and the spirit of the Olympics. For many athletes, the experiences they have in the Olympic Village are just as memorable as their competitions. In this chapter, we'll explore the various aspects of the Olympic Village at the 2024 Paris Olympics, from accommodation and facilities to daily life, security and health measures, and cultural exchange programs. Let's dive into the heart of where the world's best athletes live, train, and connect during the Games.

Accommodation and Facilities for Athletes

The Olympic Village is designed to provide athletes with a comfortable and supportive environment where they can relax, prepare, and recover between their events. Here's a look at the accommodations and facilities that make the Olympic Village a home away from home for the world's top athletes:

1. Athlete Accommodation

Athletes are housed in modern, purpose-built apartments that are designed to meet their specific needs. Each apartment is furnished to provide a comfortable living space, with amenities that help athletes feel at home.

- **Example:** Each apartment includes bedrooms, a living area, a kitchenette, and a bathroom. The design prioritizes comfort and functionality, with features such as high-quality bedding, ample storage space, and blackout curtains to ensure restful sleep.

2. Dining Facilities

The Olympic Village features several dining halls that cater to a wide variety of dietary needs and preferences. From local French cuisine to international dishes, athletes have access to nutritious meals that support their training and recovery.

- Example: Dining halls offer a diverse menu that includes options for vegetarians, vegans, and athletes with specific dietary restrictions. There are also stations dedicated to different cuisines, such as Italian, Asian, and Mediterranean, ensuring that everyone can find something they enjoy.

3. Training and Fitness Centers

To help athletes stay in peak condition, the Olympic Village is equipped with state-of-the-art training and fitness facilities. These centers provide everything athletes need to maintain their training routines and recover from their events.

- **Example:** The training centers include fully equipped gyms, swimming pools, running tracks, and specialized areas for sports like weightlifting and gymnastics. Additionally, there are recovery facilities such as ice baths, saunas, and massage rooms.

4. Medical and Health Services

Comprehensive medical and health services are available 24/7 in the Olympic Village. These services ensure that athletes receive immediate care for any injuries or health concerns, helping them stay healthy and perform at their best.

- *Example:* The medical center in the Village is staffed with doctors, physiotherapists, and other healthcare professionals who specialize in sports medicine. Services include injury treatment, physical therapy, and general health consultations.

5. Recreational and Social Spaces

Beyond their training and competition, athletes need time to relax and unwind. The Olympic Village includes recreational and social spaces where athletes can socialize, watch events, and participate in leisure activities.

- *Example:* Recreational facilities include lounges with big-screen TVs, game rooms with table tennis and pool tables, and outdoor spaces for relaxation. There are also cafes and social hubs where athletes can meet and interact with their peers from around the world.

6. Transportation Services

Efficient and reliable transportation is crucial for athletes to get to and from their events on time. The Olympic Village provides a range of transportation services, including shuttles and dedicated lanes, to ensure smooth and timely travel.

- ***Example:*** Shuttle buses run on a regular schedule, transporting athletes to competition venues, training facilities, and other key locations. Additionally, there are bike-sharing stations and pedestrian paths for convenient on-site mobility.

Daily Life in the Olympic Village

Life in the Olympic Village is a unique experience that goes beyond the daily grind of training and competition. It's a place where athletes from different countries and disciplines come together, creating a vibrant and dynamic community. Here's a glimpse into daily life in the Village.

1. Morning Routine

For many athletes, the day starts early with a focus on preparing for their training or competition. A typical morning might include a healthy breakfast, followed by a session in the gym or a visit to the training center.

- ***Example:*** An athlete might start their day with a balanced breakfast in the dining hall, choosing from a variety of healthy options such as fresh fruits, whole grains, and protein-rich foods. After breakfast, they head to the training center for a morning workout or a practice session.

2. Training Sessions

Training is a crucial part of an athlete's daily routine in the Olympic Village. The facilities are designed to accommodate the specific needs of different sports, allowing athletes to maintain their performance levels.

- *Example:* Swimmers might spend their mornings in the pool, working on their strokes and endurance, while track athletes might focus on sprints or technique drills on the running track. The training sessions are often intense, with athletes pushing themselves to their limits.

3. Meal Times

Nutrition is a key component of an athlete's regimen, and meal times in the Village are designed to provide the right balance of nutrients. Athletes can choose from a wide variety of dishes, ensuring they get the energy they need for their activities.

- *Example:* Lunch might include a mix of lean proteins, complex carbohydrates, and plenty of vegetables. Athletes can customize their meals to meet their dietary needs, whether they're focusing on muscle recovery, energy replenishment, or maintaining a balanced diet.

4. Rest and Recovery

Recovery is just as important as training, and athletes have access to a range of facilities and services to help them recover effectively. This includes physical therapy, massage, and leisure activities to relax their minds and bodies.

- Example: After a morning of intense training, an athlete might visit the recovery center for a massage or use the ice baths to reduce muscle soreness. They might also spend time in the lounge, watching TV or reading a book to unwind.

5. Social Activities

The Olympic Village is not just about training and competition; it's also a place where athletes can socialize and build friendships. There are numerous social activities and events designed to foster camaraderie and cultural exchange.

- Example: In the evenings, athletes might gather in the common areas to watch the day's competitions on big screens, participate in organized social events, or simply hang out and chat with fellow athletes from around the world.

6. Evening Wind-Down

Evenings in the Olympic Village are a time for relaxation and preparation for the next day. Athletes often use this time to review their performance, plan their training, and get a good night's sleep.

- Example: After dinner, an athlete might spend some quiet time reflecting on their day and setting goals for the next. They might also connect with their coaches for feedback and strategy discussions before heading to bed for a restful sleep.

Security and Health Measures

Ensuring the safety and well-being of athletes is a top priority at the Olympic Village. Comprehensive security and health measures are in place to provide a secure and healthy environment for everyone.

1. Security Protocols

The Olympic Village is equipped with robust security measures to protect athletes and staff. This includes perimeter security, access control, and continuous monitoring to prevent any unauthorized access or incidents.

- Example: Security personnel are stationed at all entry points, and athletes and staff must use accredited passes to enter the Village. Surveillance cameras and security patrols ensure that the area is monitored around the clock.

2. Health and Hygiene

Maintaining high standards of health and hygiene is crucial, especially in a setting where athletes are in close contact. The Olympic Village has implemented rigorous health protocols to prevent the spread of illnesses and ensure a safe environment.

- Example: Hand sanitizing stations are located throughout the Village, and regular cleaning and disinfection procedures are carried out in common areas. Athletes are encouraged to

follow personal hygiene practices, such as frequent handwashing and wearing masks in crowded spaces.

3. Medical Services

Comprehensive medical services are available in the Olympic Village to address any health issues that arise. This includes emergency care, routine medical check-ups, and specialized sports medicine services.

- **Example:** The medical center is staffed with doctors, nurses, and physiotherapists who can provide immediate treatment for injuries, illnesses, and other health concerns. Advanced medical equipment and facilities ensure that athletes receive top-quality care.

4. COVID-19 Precautions

Given the ongoing concerns about COVID-19, specific precautions have been put in place to protect athletes from the virus. These measures include testing, quarantine protocols, and vaccination requirements.

- **Example:** Athletes and staff are required to undergo regular COVID-19 testing, and anyone showing symptoms or testing positive is isolated and provided with appropriate medical care. Vaccination is strongly encouraged, and vaccination status is monitored as part of the entry requirements.

5. Emergency Response

In the event of an emergency, well-coordinated response plans are in place to ensure swift and effective action. This includes procedures for medical emergencies, security incidents, and other potential crises.

- **Example:** Emergency drills are conducted regularly to prepare staff and athletes for various scenarios, ensuring that everyone knows the protocols and can respond quickly and calmly in an actual emergency.

Cultural Exchange Programs

One of the most enriching aspects of the Olympic Village is the opportunity for cultural exchange. Athletes from different countries and backgrounds come together, sharing their cultures and learning from one another. The Paris 2024 Olympics have organized several programs to facilitate these exchanges.

1. Cultural Events and Festivals

Throughout the Games, various cultural events and festivals are organized in the Olympic Village. These events showcase the host country's culture as well as the diverse cultures of the participating nations.

- **Example:** A French cultural festival featuring traditional music, dance, and cuisine might be held in the Village, allowing athletes to experience the rich heritage of the host country. Similarly, athletes are encouraged to share their own cultures through performances and displays.

2. Language Exchange Programs

Language exchange programs provide athletes with the opportunity to learn new languages and practice their language skills with native speakers. These programs foster communication and understanding among athletes from different parts of the world.

- ***Example:*** Language exchange sessions, where athletes can pair up to teach each other phrases and basics of their native languages, are organized regularly. This not only enhances communication but also creates lasting friendships.

3. Culinary Exchange

Food is a universal language, and culinary exchange programs allow athletes to share their traditional dishes and learn about the cuisines of other countries. These programs often include cooking demonstrations and tasting sessions.

- ***Example:*** Athletes can participate in cooking classes where they learn to prepare traditional French dishes such as croissants or ratatouille. Likewise, they can share their own recipes and culinary traditions with fellow athletes, creating a multicultural dining experience.

4. Art and Craft Workshops

Art and craft workshops offer a creative outlet for athletes and provide a platform for cultural exchange. These workshops allow athletes to express themselves and share their cultural heritage through art.

- **Example:** Workshops might include painting, pottery, or traditional crafts from various cultures. Athletes can create artworks that reflect their cultural backgrounds and learn new techniques from artists around the world.

5. *Cultural Dialogues and Discussions*

Organized discussions and forums provide a platform for athletes to share their experiences and perspectives on various cultural topics. These dialogues promote mutual understanding and respect among participants.

- **Example:** Panel discussions on topics such as cultural identity, global citizenship, and the role of sports in bridging cultural divides are held regularly. Athletes can share their personal stories and engage in meaningful conversations with their peers.

6. *Performances and Showcases*

Performances and cultural showcases are a highlight of life in the Olympic Village. Athletes can participate in or enjoy performances that include music, dance, theater, and other cultural expressions.

- **Example:** An evening showcase might feature a mix of performances, such as a traditional Japanese tea ceremony, a Brazilian samba dance, and an American jazz concert. These events celebrate the diversity of the Olympic community and provide entertainment and enrichment.

Conclusion

The Olympic Village at the 2024 Paris Olympics is a microcosm of the world, bringing together athletes from diverse cultures and backgrounds to live, train, and celebrate together. The accommodations and facilities provide a comfortable and supportive environment, while daily life in the Village is enriched by opportunities for socialization, relaxation, and cultural exchange.

Security and health measures ensure that athletes can focus on their performance without worrying about their safety and well-being. The cultural exchange programs foster a spirit of unity and understanding, allowing athletes to learn from each other and build lasting connections.

As we look forward to the Games, the Olympic Village stands as a testament to the power of sports to bring people together and create a global community. Whether through shared meals, cultural performances, or simply living side by side, the experiences in the Olympic Village will leave a lasting impact on all who participate.

CHAPTER TWELVE
Appendices

In this chapter, we will explore the appendices of our book on the 2024 Paris Olympics. Here, you'll find essential information that will enhance your understanding and enjoyment of the Games. Whether you're looking to familiarize yourself with Olympic terminology, explore the list of participating countries, plan your viewing schedule, or quickly locate information in the book, this chapter has you covered. Let's dive into these helpful resources together.

Glossary of Terms

The Olympics have their own unique language, filled with specific terms and phrases. This glossary will help you navigate the terminology of the Games and ensure you understand everything that's happening.

A

- **Athlete's Village:** Another term for the Olympic Village, where athletes stay during the Games.

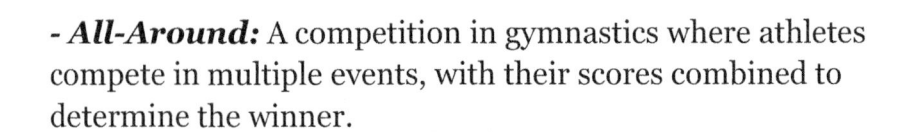

- **All-Around:** A competition in gymnastics where athletes compete in multiple events, with their scores combined to determine the winner.

B

- **Bronze Medal:** The medal awarded to the athlete or team that finishes in third place.

C

- **Ceremony:** The formal events that open and close the Olympic Games, including the Parade of Nations and the lighting/extinguishing of the Olympic flame.

- **Combined Events:** Competitions that require athletes to participate in multiple sports or events, such as the decathlon and heptathlon.

D

- **Decathlon:** A track and field combined event for men, consisting of ten different disciplines.

- **Doping:** The use of banned substances or methods to enhance athletic performance.

E

- **Event:** A specific competition within a sport, such as the 100m sprint in athletics or the freestyle swimming race.

F

- **Final:** The last race or competition in an event, which determines the medal winners.

- **Flagbearer:** The athlete chosen to carry their country's flag during the Parade of Nations at the opening and closing ceremonies.

G

- **Gold Medal:** The medal awarded to the athlete or team that finishes in first place.

H

- ***Heat:*** A preliminary race in a track or swimming event to determine which athletes advance to the next round.

I

- ***IOC (International Olympic Committee):*** The organization responsible for overseeing the Olympic Games and the Olympic Movement.

J

- ***Judging Panel:*** The group of officials who score performances in judged sports, such as gymnastics and diving.

K

- ***Keirin:*** A track cycling event where riders follow a pacing motorcycle before sprinting to the finish.

L

- ***Long Jump:*** An athletics event where athletes run and jump as far as possible into a sandpit.

M

- **Medley:** A swimming event where athletes swim four different strokes in a single race.

- **Modern Pentathlon:** An Olympic sport comprising fencing, swimming, equestrian show jumping, pistol shooting, and cross-country running.

N

- **National Olympic Committee (NOC):** The organization responsible for coordinating Olympic activities in each country.

O

- **Olympiad:** The four-year period between Olympic Games.

- **Olympic Charter:** The set of rules and guidelines for the organization and operation of the Olympic Movement.

P

- **Paralympics:** A major international multi-sport event involving athletes with a range of disabilities, held immediately following the Olympics.

- **Pole Vault:** An athletics event where athletes use a pole to vault over a high bar.

Q

- **Qualifying Round:** A preliminary competition to determine which athletes advance to the final rounds.

R

- **Relay:** A team race in track or swimming where each team member runs or swims a segment of the race.

S

- **Silver Medal:** The medal awarded to the athlete or team that finishes in second place.

- **Sprint:** A short-distance race in athletics or swimming, typically focused on speed.

T

- ***Track and Field:*** A collection of athletic events that take place on a running track and a field area.

- ***Triathlon:*** A multi-sport event consisting of swimming, cycling, and running.

U

- Unified Sports: Competitions that include athletes with and without intellectual disabilities competing together.

V

- Venue: The location where a specific Olympic event takes place.

W

- ***Weightlifting:*** A sport where athletes lift heavy weights in two types of lifts: the snatch and the clean and jerk.

- **World Record:** The best performance recorded globally in a particular event.

X

- **X-Country:** Short for cross-country, used in events like cross-country running or skiing.

Y

- **Youth Olympics:** An international multi-sport event for young athletes aged 14 to 18, held every four years.

Z

- **Zonal Qualifiers:** Regional competitions that determine qualification for the Olympics.

Detailed Event Schedule

Planning your viewing schedule is essential to catching all the excitement of the Olympics. Here's a detailed event schedule for the 2024 Paris Olympics, organized by sport and date:

Day 1: July 26, 2024

- Opening Ceremony: Stade de France, 20:00

Day 2: July 27, 2024

- Archery: Men's and Women's Individual Ranking Round
- Basketball: Men's Preliminary Round
- Cycling (Road): Men's Road Race
- Gymnastics (Artistic): Men's Qualification
- Swimming: Preliminary Heats

Day 3: July 28, 2024

- Archery: Mixed Team Event
- Basketball: Women's Preliminary Round
- Cycling (Road): Women's Road Race
- Gymnastics (Artistic): Women's Qualification
- Swimming: Preliminary Heats and Finals

Day 4: July 29, 2024

- Archery: Men's Team Event

- Basketball: Men's Preliminary Round
- Gymnastics (Artistic): Men's Team Final
- Swimming: Preliminary Heats and Finals
- Tennis: Men's and Women's Singles First Round

Day 5: July 30, 2024

- Archery: Women's Team Event
- Basketball: Women's Preliminary Round
- Diving: Men's 3m Springboard Preliminary
- Gymnastics (Artistic): Women's Team Final
- Swimming: Preliminary Heats and Finals
- Tennis: Men's and Women's Singles Second Round

Day 6: July 31, 2024

- Archery: Men's Individual Rounds
- Basketball: Men's Preliminary Round
- Diving: Men's 3m Springboard Final
- Fencing: Women's Foil Individual
- Gymnastics (Artistic): Men's All-Around Final
- Swimming: Preliminary Heats and Finals
- Tennis: Men's and Women's Singles Third Round

Day 7: August 1, 2024

- Archery: Women's Individual Rounds
- Basketball: Women's Preliminary Round
- Diving: Women's 10m Platform Preliminary
- Fencing: Men's Epee Individual
- Gymnastics (Artistic): Women's All-Around Final
- Swimming: Preliminary Heats and Finals
- Tennis: Men's and Women's Singles Quarterfinals

Day 8: August 2, 2024

- Archery: Mixed Team Final
- Basketball: Men's Preliminary Round
- Diving: Women's 10m Platform Final
- Fencing: Women's Sabre Individual
- Gymnastics (Artistic): Men's Event Finals
- Swimming: Preliminary Heats and Finals
- Tennis: Men's and Women's Singles Semifinals

Day 9: August 3, 2024

- Archery: Men's Individual Final
- Athletics: Men's 100m Heats
- Basketball: Women's Preliminary Round

- Diving: Men's 10m Platform Preliminary
- Fencing: Men's Foil Team
- Gymnastics (Artistic): Women's Event Finals
- Swimming: Preliminary Heats and Finals
- Tennis: Men's and Women's Singles Finals

Day 10: August 4, 2024

- Archery: Women's Individual Final
- Athletics: Women's 100m Heats
- Basketball: Men's Preliminary Round
- Diving: Men's 10m Platform Final
- Fencing: Women's Epee Team
- Swimming: Preliminary Heats and Finals
- Tennis: Mixed Doubles Final

Day 11: August 5, 2024

- Athletics: Men's and Women's 100m Finals
- Basketball: Women's Preliminary Round
- Cycling (Track): Men's and Women's Sprint
- Fencing: Men's Sabre Team
- Swimming: Preliminary Heats and Finals

Day 12: August 6, 2024

- Athletics: Men's 200m Heats
- Basketball: Men's Preliminary Round
- Cycling (Track): Men's and Women's Keirin
- Fencing: Women's Foil Team
- Swimming: Preliminary Heats and Finals

Day 13: August 7, 2024

- Athletics: Women's 200m Heats
- Basketball: Women's Preliminary Round
- Cycling (Track): Men's and Women's Omnium
- Swimming: Preliminary Heats and Finals

Day 14: August 8, 2024

- Athletics: Men's and Women's 4x100m Relay Heats
- Basketball: Men's Quarterfinals
- Cycling (Track): Men's and Women's Team Pursuit
- Swimming: Preliminary Heats and Finals

Day 15: August 9, 2024

- Athletics: Men's and Women's 4x100m Relay Finals
- Basketball: Women's Semifinals
- Cycling (Track): Men's and Women's Madison

- Swimming: Preliminary Heats and Finals

Day 16: August 10, 2024

- Athletics: Men's 1500m Final
- Basketball: Men's Semifinals
- Cycling (Track): Men's and Women's Points Race
- Swimming: Preliminary Heats and Finals

Day 17: August 11, 2024

- Athletics: Women's 1500m Final
- Basketball: Women's Final
- Cycling (Track): Men's and Women's Scratch Race
- Swimming: Preliminary Heats and Finals

Day 18: August 12, 2024

- Athletics: Men's and Women's Marathon
- Basketball: Men's Final
- Closing Ceremony: Stade de France, 20:00

CONCLUSION

As we turn the final pages of "Olympic Games Paris 2024: The Ultimate Handbook for the 2024 Summer Olympics," we're left buzzing with excitement for what's just around the corner.

Picture it: on the 26th of July, 2024, the world will gather in the City of Lights, ready to witness the spectacle of a lifetime. Paris will transform into a global stage, where dreams take flight, records shatter, and heroes emerge.

We've followed the journey of athletes who have trained tirelessly, overcoming challenges and embodying the true spirit of the Olympics. Their stories have inspired us, and now, the moment we've all been waiting for is nearly here. Can you feel the anticipation? The energy? It's electric!

So, mark your calendars and get your popcorn ready. Whether you're a sports fanatic, a casual viewer, or just in it for the breathtaking opening ceremony, Paris 2024 promises to be an unforgettable experience. As we gear up for the games, let's carry forward the enthusiasm and unity that the Olympics bring.

Here's to the athletes, the fans, and the magic of the Olympics. See you in Paris!

Printed in Great Britain
by Amazon